ART AND HISTORY OF
WASHINGTON D.C.

Text by
BRUCE R. SMITH

Photographs by
ANDREA PISTOLESI

ℬℬ
BONECHI

D0521637

ey

Distribution by:
Eiron, Inc
POB 40072 Washington DC 20016
phone: (202) 966 3240
fax: (202) 244 0913

Project and editorial conception: Casa Editrice Bonechi
Publication Manager: Monica Bonechi
Picture research: Monica Bonechi
Cover, graphic design, make-up and editing: Alberto Douglas Scotti
Maps by Stefano Benini

Text by Bruce R. Smith

© Copyright 1997 by Casa Editrice Bonechi - Florence - Italy

E-mail:bonechi@bonechi.it
Internet:www.bonechi.it

New York Address:
255 Centre Street - 6th Floor - New York, NY 10013 - Tel.: (212)343-1464 - Fax: (212)343-8045

*Photographs from the archives of Casa Editrice Bonechi taken by
Andrea Pistolesi,
except pages 82-83, courtesy of The White House Historical Association and page 103 below ,© Fred J. Maroon.*

ISBN 88-8029-762-7

* * *

INTRODUCTION

International cosmopolis, capital of the United States of America, national center for commerce and the arts, collage of distinctive neighborhoods: Washington, D. C., is all of these places, all at the same time. Riding the city's Metrorail system, you might find yourself sitting next to one of the legislators, lawyers, or lobbyists for which Washington is notorious, but just as easily your fellow passenger might be an economist at the World Bank, or a space scientist, or an authority on African art. Settling in for a performance of the National Symphony at the Kennedy Center, you might overhear the conversation of a diplomat from France, or a specialist in Native American cultures from the Smithsonian, or a student from one of the area's twenty-some colleges and universities. Strolling along the banks of the Potomac River in West Potomac Park, you might spot Capitol Hill staffers tossing a frisbee, workers from the Organization of American States playing soccer, fourth-generation native Washingtonians fishing, families from all over the country enjoying a picnic. When it comes time to eat, there are not only world-class restaurants to choose from but a wide range of smaller places serving the cuisines that have arrived along with new citizens who now call the Washington area home: Afghani, Bolivian, Cambodian, Salvadorian, Ethiopian, Korean, Nicaraguan, Vietnamese. Amid it all, you can find the accents, architectural styles, food, and folkways that make Washington a city of the Piedmont plateau, situated halfway between the Chesapeake Bay to the east and the Appalachian Mountains to the west.

For untold centuries, the land where Washington now stands was hunted, farmed, and fished by Algonquian-speaking Native Americans. Suggestions of the wooded landscape these people knew can be appreciated today in Rock Creek Park. The park runs through the entire length of the northwest part of the city down to the Potomac River, passing by one of the tribes' major soapstone quarries along Piney Branch Parkway. Although Spanish ships explored the Chesapeake Bay in the late sixteenth century, it was not until 1608 that Europeans first arrived in the Potomac valley, when Captain John Smith sailed up the river, possibly as far as the head of navigation at Little Falls, four and a half miles northwest of what is today Arlington Memorial Bridge. Along the way he noted the presence of a Native American settlement called Nacothtank on the present-day site of Anacostia in Southeast Washington. In 1632 Henry Fleete, a fur trader, made the same journey, stopping off at a settlement he called Tohoga, probably near the present-day site of Georgetown. Fleete liked what he saw: "This place is without question the most pleasant and healthful place in all this country and most convenient for habitation, the air being temperate in summer and not violent in winter." Anglo settlement followed these exploratory missions, mostly in huge plantations along both sides of the river. Native people were quickly decimated, in Thomas Jefferson's tactful phrasing, "by smallpox, spiritous liquors, and abridgement of territory." When merchants founded two port cities, Alexandria in Virginia and Georgetown in Maryland, to handle the shipping and commerical needs of the Potomac plantations, they little dreamed that both places would someday be swallowed up in a huge metropolis. Today Georgetown and Alexandria, two of Washington's most atmospheric neighborhoods, retain dozens of reminders of the colonial past. The event that changed the region forever came in 1790, seven years after the colonies achieved independence from Great Britain, when the Potomac River region was chosen as the site for the capital of the newly formed United States of America. Prophetically enough, it was a political compromise that determined the location, much farther south than anyone from Boston, New York, or Philadelphia would have liked. Two political enemies, Thomas Jefferson and Alexander Hamilton, worked it all out over dinner, managing in the process to resolve— for the time being, at least—an economic stand-off between the northern colonies and the southern that threatened the new republic's very existence. The exact site, at the confluence of the Potomac River with the Anacostia River, was chosen by George Washington. All sorts of people had a hand in making the new city. An African-American mathematician, Benjamin Banneker, joined Andrew Ellicott, a surveyor, in mapping the site. The design itself, a grid

The heroic proportions of the **Washington Monument**, a white marble shaft extending 555 feet into the sky, and the personal pathos of the **Vietnam Veterans Memorial**, a low black marble wall inscribed with the name of every American killed in the Vietnam war, are two of the features that make **the Mall** the "seat of the national conscience."

bisected by broad avenues that converge on circles and squares, was drawn by Major Pierre Charles L'Enfant, a French engineer who had come to America with the Marquis de Lafayette and had fought in the Revolutionary War.

Washington, as the new seat of government came to be called the first year, was one of the first great cities since Roman times to be planned from the top down. L'Enfant's design was based on principles both aesthetic and practical. "Lines or avenues of direct communication" would serve, in L'Enfant's words, "to connect the separate and most distant objects with the principal, and to preserve through the whole a reciprocity of sight." Such vistas not only produce an imposing effect; they also make it easier to control mobs, as Baron Haussmann realized when he redesigned Paris along similar lines sixty years after Washington was laid out. (Conventional wisdom has it that Washington was inspired by Paris.) The most serious challenge to Washington's development came during the War of 1812, when British troops invaded what General Robert Ross called "this harbor of Yankee democracy" and set fire to the Capitol, the White House, and other public buildings. Afterwards, fully a third of the Congress voted to move the capital somewhere else rather than rebuild. Reconstruction did take place, but as late as 1842 Charles Dickens, surveying vacant lots and rough-

The **Lincoln Memorial** presides over the western end of the Mall.

4

The **Reflecting Pool** catches images (left to right) of the **Capitol,** the **Washington Monument,** the **Library of Congress** and the **Smithsonian Castle.**

and-ready buildings at every turn, could dismiss "the City of Magnificent Distances" as "the City of Magnificent Intentions." Real growth began in the 1850s and has never stopped since. Through it all L'Enfant's plan has been preserved and extended. Original features of the plan like the Capitol and the White House were complemented in the nineteenth century by addition of the Washington Monument, the Old Post Office, and the Smithsonian Castle, at the turn of the twentieth century by the mansions of Dupont Circle and Embassy Row, in the 1930s and 40s by the Federal Triangle, the National Gallery of Art, and the Lincoln and Jefferson Memorials, and in the late twentieth century by the Kennedy Center for the Performing Arts, the Air and Space Museum, the East Building of the National Gallery of Art, the Holocaust Museum, and the Vietnam and Korean war memorials. Scores of new office buildings in downtown Washington and in the West End, all of them at the statutory maximum height established by Congress in 1910, have uniformly raised L'Enfant's grand design into three dimensions. During its two centuries of existence Washington has long since outgrown the ten-mile square envisioned by its founders, spilling over into the adjacent states of Maryland and Virginia. Today the Washington metropolitan area is home to more than four million people in an area that covers 3,957 square miles.

*The two-mile sweep of **the Mall** constitutes one of the world's most famous urban spaces. Overlooking the prospect (lower right) is the **U.S. Capitol.***

THE MALL

Parade route, rallying ground, outdoor pantheon to America's national heroes, sports field, fairground, seat of the national conscience: the Mall democratically combines all these functions in one of North America's great public spaces. L'Enfant had imagined the Mall as a "place of general resort," to be lined with theaters, assembly halls, academies, and "all sort of places as may be attractive to the learned and afford diversion to the idle." A single grand avenue 400 feet wide, lined with grand houses, was to run down from the Capitol to the site of the Washington Monument, where it would intersect with another broad axis of open space running from the White House down to the Potomac. In 1791, the river's tidal waters lapped at the foot of the monument site. How the Mall came to fulfill L'Enfant's dream is a long, eventful story. During the War of 1812 the future Mall served as a drill ground for British troops. Through the first half of the nineteenth century it remained mostly unlandscaped. The fetid waters of a canal cut the Capitol off from the Mall; tracks of the Baltimore & Pacific Railroad ran across the grounds to a station on the site of the National Gallery of Art. Erection of the Smithsonian

Castle in 1855 coincided with a scheme to landscape the Mall along picturesque lines, with groves and meandering paths. The Civil War interrupted those plans: the Mall became a massive military camp. Only at the turn of the twentieth century did L'Enfant's original design get dusted off, when the McMillan Commission, headed by Senator James McMillan of Michigan, drafted the master plan that has gradually been realized over the past hundred years. The Department of Agriculture Building (1905) was the first structure along the Mall to be erected according to the commission's plans, followed a few years later by the National Museum of Natural History (1911). Other museums of the Smithsonian Institution have arisen on sites up and down the Mall: the National Gallery of Art (1941), the National Museum of American History (1964), the National Air and Space Museum (1976). Building of the Lincoln Memorial (1911-22) extended the Mall westward across former bogs and marshes. Today the monumental space of the Mall provides a setting for "learned" and "idle" activities ranging from art appreciation to kite-flying, from protest marches to the annual Boy Scout jamboree.

The Mall Area

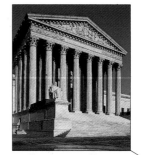

Supreme Court
(page 26)

The Capit
(page 11)

**National Gallery
West Building**
(page 31)

**National Gallery East
Building** *(page 31)*

**Museum of Natural
History. Museum
of Man** *(page 42)*

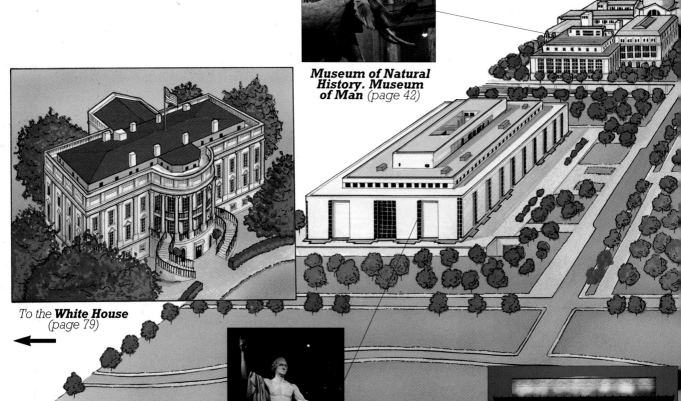

To the **White House**
(page 79)

**Museum of
American History**
(page 46)

To **Lincoln Memorial** *(page 72)*

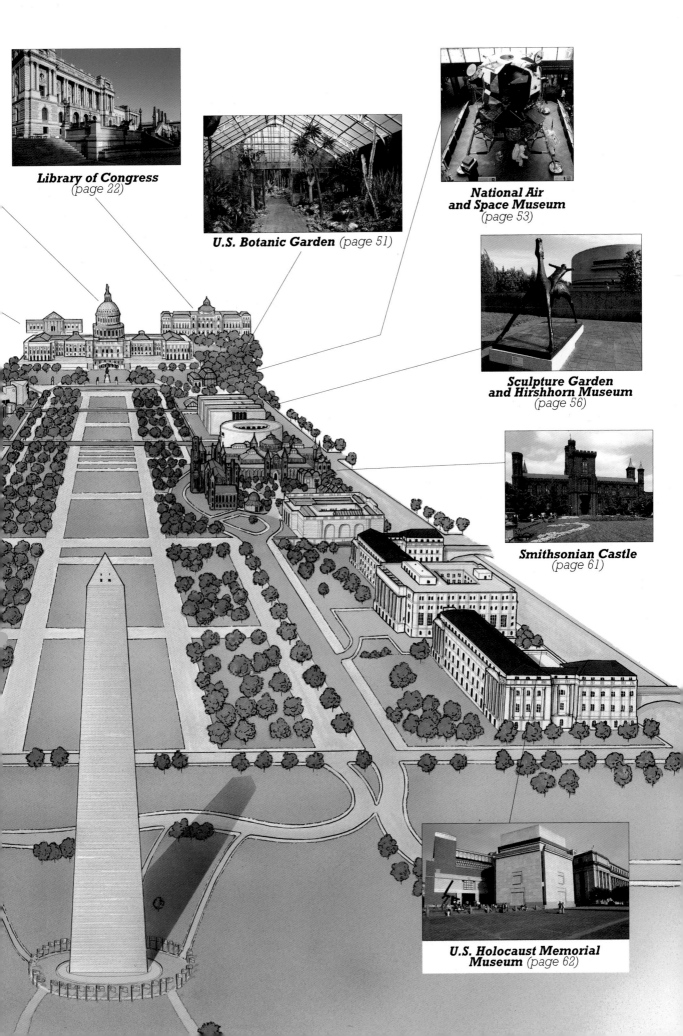

Library of Congress
(page 22)

U.S. Botanic Garden (page 51)

**National Air
and Space Museum**
(page 53)

**Sculpture Garden
and Hirshhorn Museum**
(page 56)

Smithsonian Castle
(page 61)

**U.S. Holocaust Memorial
Museum** (page 62)

The Capitol's **west facade** (left) retains the sandstone walls
of the original building, erected between 1800 and 1807. The
dome (above) was raised later, during the Civil War.

THE CAPITOL

Where does the United States of America begin?
Some might say at Philadelphia, on July 4, 1776.
But a good argument could be made that it begins on
an 88-foot rise above the Potomac formerly known
as Jenkins Hill. L'Enfant pronounced the site ''a
pedestal waiting for a monument'' and chose it for
the centerpiece to his design for the new capital city
in 1791. From the Capitol broad avenues radiate in
all directions, just as L'Enfant planned, drawing
attention from all quarters of the city to this central
point. It is here that the central axes of the city cross,
dividing the City of Washington into the four
quadrants by which residents and visitors take their
bearings: Northeast, Southeast, Southwest,
Northwest. Literally as well as figuratively, the
avenues converging on the Capitol draw the nation
toward the building in which the federation's affairs
are democratically decided: Maryland Avenue
comes in from the northeast, New Jersey and
Delaware from the north, Pennsylvania from the
northwest. Standing on the Capitol's expansive west
terrace, visitors can look down the Mall, across the
Potomac River, and beyond the hills of Arlington,
Virginia, toward the vast continent that the new
nation eventually came to occupy. In its present form

the Capitol stands as an heroic symbol of the states'
commitment to union. Through the whole of the Civil
War work continued on extensions to the building
that had begun in the 1850s. ''If people see the
Capitol going on,'' Lincoln observed, ''... it is a sign
we intend the Union shall go on.'' The dome was
raised in the depths of the war, reaching completion
on December 2, 1863, when Thomas Crawford's
statue of ''Freedom'' was lifted into place amid
volleys of ceremonial gun fire from the twelve forts
that encircled the beleaguered city.

The Capitol as it stands today still presents the
simple three-part arrangement envisioned by
William Thornton, the physician and amateur
architect who won the competition for the building's
design in 1793. Facing the east facade, with the
Supreme Court and the Library of Congress behind
them, visitors can distinguish three clear units: a
pavilion for the Senate on the right, a pavilion for the
House of Representatives on the left, and a central
rotunda. Though the idea of three components has
remained the same, the structure of the building has
passed through four phases of development.

The **first phase** saw the realization of Thornton's
basic design, with help from Benjamin Henry

The **west terraces** of the Capitol (left) were laid out by Frederick Law Olmsted, designer of New York's Central Park.

The **Ulysses S. Grant Memorial** (this page) is the second largest equestrian statue in the world, yielding place only to the Victor Emmanuel Monument in Rome.

Latrobe, the first American-born professional architect. The cornerstone was set in place on November 18, 1793, by George Washington. The silver trowel that he used still exists and has continued to be used for laying cornerstones to important buildings in the Washington area. First a pavilion for the Senate (1800) and then one for the House (1807) were completed, linked by a covered wooden walkway in place of Thornton's unbuilt rotunda. The Senate and the House pavilions, each with its own small dome, are visible today to the right and the left of the central portico. Nineteenth-century extensions have turned them into links in a much larger design. It was Thornton and Latrobe's building that British soldiers put to the torch in 1814, using books from the Library of Congress as kindling. After the war work began on the **second phase** of the Capitol's construction, a restoration of Thornton

The **east facade** of the Capitol shows all four phases of the building's construction.

and Latrobe's House and Senate pavilions, with the addition of a central rotunda that featured a large, 55-foot-high dome, designed by Charles Bulfinch along the lines of the dome he had supplied for the Massachusetts Statehouse in Boston. The result charmed even the usually acerbic Frances Trollope, who confessed to her British readers in 1832 that "the beauty and majesty of the American capitol might defy an abler pen than mine."

In the **third phase** of construction the Capitol assumed its present form. The need for more space in the 1850s prompted Congress to commission some extensions. Thomas U. Walter designed the wings for the House (completed 1857) and the Senate (1859) that are still in use today. Walter's new construction more than doubled the building's length—from 352 feet to 746 feet—making Bulfinch's dome seem much too small. A new dome, the one that still crowns the edifice, rose to take the place of Bulfinch's dome in 1863. One of the great engineering feats of the nineteenth century, the nine-million-pound dome is made up of two cast-iron shells, one set inside the other. Painted outside and in to resemble marble, the cast-iron structure is not only stronger than stone but lighter and more flexible. Calculations made shortly after its erection suggest that the metal can expand and contract by up to four inches with changes in air temperature. The ultimate inspiration for Walter's design was Michelangelo's dome for St. Peter's in Rome (1546-90), but more immediately the cast-iron dome of St. Isaac's Cathedral in St. Petersburg (1842).

In the **fourth and final phase** of construction (1959-60) the central pavilion's eastern front was brought forward 32 feet 6 inches, a refinement Walter had proposed a century earlier.

*The Capitol **grounds,** landscaped by Frederick Law Olmsted, are particularly beautiful in spring.*

*The cast-iron **dome** of the U. S. Capitol is one of the great engineering feats of the nineteenth century. It is topped by Thomas Crawford's 19-foot **statue of Freedom.***

The Capitol's interior spaces, all of them sumptuously decorated, are dominated by the Great Rotunda, 95 feet 8 inches in diameter and 183 feet high. Under canopy of the dome is a 6000-square-foot fresco of "The Apotheosis of Washington," showing the first president attended by figures embodying Liberty and Victory and the Thirteen Original States, along with War, Agriculture, Mechanics, Commerce, Maritime Operations, and the Arts and Sciences. The artist, Costantino Brumidi (1805-1880), had worked in the Vatican before emigrating to America. He died while working on another part of the rotunda's decoration, the grisaille frieze that runs around the walls 75 feet above the floor. Among the huge paintings at floor level are four by John Trumbull (1756-1843), an aide to General Washington and a participant in some of the epic events shown in the paintings.
 North of the Great Rotunda, the Old Senate

Costantino Brumidi's fresco **The Apotheosis of Washington** *crowns the dome's interior.*

Statuary Hall (above) and the **Old Senate Chamber**
(below) are two features of the original building.

Chamber was the site of legendary speeches by John C. Calhoun, Henry Clay, and Daniel Webster. The Supreme Court sat in this room from 1860 until it moved across the street in 1935. In the small rotunda just outside can be seen one of the Capitol's most charming features, columns designed by Latrobe that substitute indigenous American plants—maize, tobacco, and cotton—for the acanthus leaves of classical Corinthian columns. Beyond lies the new Senate Chamber. South of the Rotunda, enroute to the new House of Representatives Chamber, is to be found the lower house's old chamber, which has served since 1864 as Statuary Hall. Each state of the union has sent to the Capitol likenesses of two of its prominent citizens. One from each state is displayed in this room. A bronze star on the floor marks the spot where former President John Quincy Adams collapsed during a fatal stroke in 1848.

LIBRARY OF CONGRESS

A rugged granite exterior, looking more than a little like Charles Garnier's Paris Opera House, contains some of Washington's most sumptuous interiors. Created by an act of Congress in 1800, the library started out as a reference collection strictly for the use of senators and congressmen, but by the time it moved into its present main quarters in 1897 it had become, in effect, the American equivalent of the British Library or the Bibliothèque Nationale. The interior proclaims the institution's command over the empire of learning. In the main entrance hall, a huge stained-glass skylight illuminates the richly colored mosaics that cover the vaults of the ceilings and the expanse of the floors. Sculpted putti representing various arts and sciences (among them, Electrical Engineering, with a telephone) escort visitors up a marble staircase to a view of the allegorical spectacle's climax in the main reading room, a rotunda 100 feet in diameter under a dome 160 feet

*The pompous **exterior** of the Library of Congress (this page) has had its critics, but the building's sumptuous **interior** (right) dazzles most visitors.*

high. Computer terminals have replaced the concentric card catalogue cases of the original design—a technological necessity in a library that now contains more than 75 million items on 350 miles of bookshelves. The library occupies not only the landmark Jefferson Building but two adjacent structures: the Art-Deco Adams Building (1939) and the post-modern Madison Building (1980).

Acres of **carving, gilding, fresco,** *and* **mosaic** *(this page) reach a climax in the library's* **main reading room** *(right).*

*Ancient Roman design principles and American idealism meet in the **Supreme Court's entrance portico.***

*Historical figures, including a portrait of the building's architect, mingle with allegorical abstractions in the Supreme Court's **sculptural program** (next page).*

SUPREME COURT

Headquarters of the judicial branch of the federal government, as the Capitol is headquarters of the legislative branch and the White House of the executive branch, the Supreme Court occupies a gleaming white marble building just across from the east front of the Capitol. With its magnificent Corinthian columns, the building resembles a Roman temple—but a temple with a thoroughly modern, thoroughly American dedication to "Equal Justice Under Law," as an inscription over the porch proclaims. On the pediment above, sculpted icons of Liberty, Order, and Authority are flanked by likenesses of several real-life personages standing in for Council and Research. Among them are William Howard Taft, the only man to serve both as President of the United States and as Chief Justice of the Supreme Court, and Cass Gilbert, the building's architect. Large sculpted figures by James Earle Fraser on each side of the steps portray, on the left, Contemplation of Justice and, on the right, Authority of Law. After occupying various temporary sites, including the Old Senate Chamber of the Capitol, the court moved into its own building in 1935.

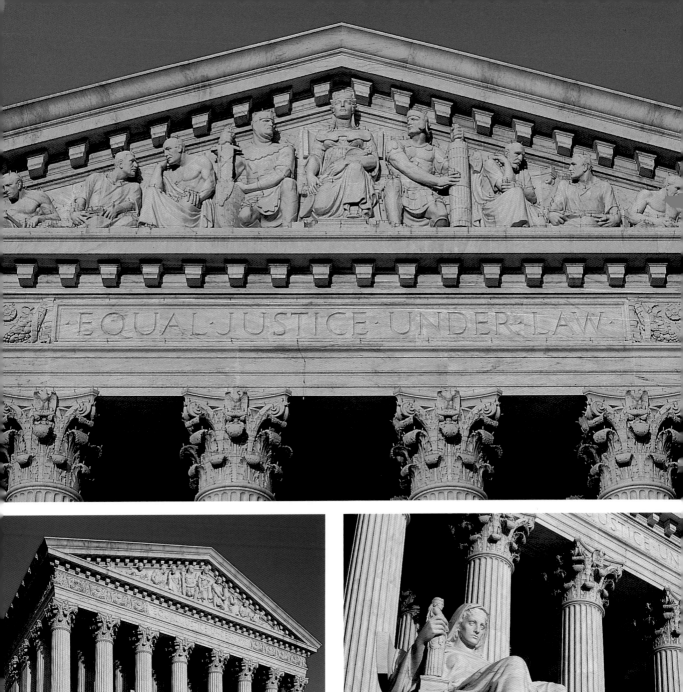

EQUAL·JUSTICE·UNDER·LAW·

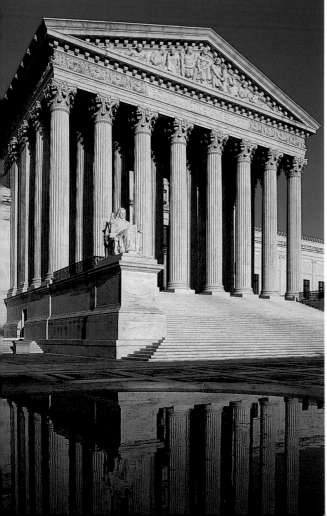

Lorado Taft's **Columbus Memorial Fountain** *(1908)*
dominates Union Station's entrance plaza.

*The Baths of Diocletian in Rome inspired the
station's* **vaulted interior.**

UNION STATION

Monument to memorable events in history, hub of transportation, shopping mall, entertainment complex: the newly refurbished Union Station magnificently combines all these functions. From the moment it was built in 1908 to consolidate several formerly separate railroad terminals (hence the name), Union Station has provided a gateway and a departure point for presidents, visiting heads of state, movie stars, martyred heroes, and sports teams, not to mention thousands upon thousands of soldiers in the first and second world wars and literally millions of inauguration visitors and protest marchers. Among the arriving dignitaries have been Charles Lindburgh, Mary Pickford, Georges Clémenceau, Winston Churchill, Queen Elizabeth II, Nikita Krushchev, Emperor Haile Selassie of Ethiopa, and The Beatles; among the departing dignitaries, Franklin D. Roosevelt, whose body was put aboard a train for Hyde Park, New York, in 1945. Though fewer trains a day pull in and out of the station today than the 200 that did so in the heyday of rail travel in

the 1920s and 30s, Union Station is still busy with commuters and passengers bound for places along the Washington-to-Boston corridor. Many more visitors come for the shops, restaurants, and movie theaters that fill the vaulted spaces of this Beaux-Arts version of the ancient Roman Baths of Diocletian. The architect was Daniel H. Burnham, director of works for the 1893 Columbian Exhibition in Chicago. Christopher Columbus, whose 1492 voyage inspired the Chicago exhibition, presides over Union Station's entrance plaza in a monumental fountain designed by Lorado Taft. After passing through the triumphal arches of the portico, visitors arrive in one of Washington's great public spaces. A gigantic barrel vault, deeply coffered and tricked out with gold leaf, sweeps over the two million cubic feet of the former main waiting room. The former first-class waiting room now houses shops, while the former Presidential Suite, originally designed for the president's private use and for receiving important visitors, has been turned into an elegant restaurant.

NATIONAL GALLERY OF ART

Youngest among the world's great museums of western art, the National Gallery owes its existence to the vision, the personal collection, and the money of a private citizen, Andrew W. Mellon (1855-1937). As early as 1841 the federal government, not by design or intent, had fallen heir to a small, miscellaneous collection of paintings that were organized as the National Institute and installed in the Patent Office building. The collection still existed in Mellon's day—it shared quarters with dinosaur bones, prodigious gems, and Native American pots in the Museum of Natural History—but Mellon had something grander in mind: a gallery of European masterpieces to rival the National Gallery of London, the Louvre, the Uffizi, the Kunsthistorisches Museum, and the Prado, in a building that would bear comparison with its European counterparts. The National Gallery of Art is the realization of Mellon's vision. Opened in 1941, the gallery's West Building joins the Jefferson Memorial (1943) as the city's last great edifices in the idiom of neo-classicism. Both were designed by John Russell Pope. On the exterior, five shades of pink marble from a quarry in Tennessee are subtly modulated from the darkest shade at ground level to the lightest on the dome. The central rotunda, modeled on the Pantheon in Rome, pivots on the light and airy figure of Mercury by the sixteenth-century Flemish-Italian master Giovanni Bologna. From the rotunda, grand corridors lead off east and west to almost a hundred galleries.

Mellon, whose family wealth came from banking and coal, coke, and iron production, had bought his first painting at the age of 27 while touring the great art capitals of Europe with another young Pittsburgh millionaire, Henry Clay Frick. Old Master paintings of the eighteenth century and earlier were the focus of Mellon's interest. By the time he donated his accumulated treasures to the nation and had built a gallery to receive them, the collection included 126 paintings and 26 pieces of sculpture—the largest such gift ever made by a single individual to a governmental entity. His most publicized acquisitions had come in 1931, when Josef Stalin sold off pictures from the collection that Catherine the Great had amassed in the Hermitage Palace in St. Petersburg.

*The generosity of private citizens, not the wealth of a royal dynasty, has produced **one of the world's most important collections of European and American art.***

*Design principles of the **Pantheon** in Rome have been realized in pink marble from Tennessee.*

Pictures from the Samuel H. Kress Collection, including "Mary Queen of Heaven" by the Netherlandish Master of the St. Lucy Legend (opposite page, below, center), form the core of the gallery's **collection of medieval and early Renaissance art.**

A late sixteenth-century **bronze Venus,** *attributed to Francesco Brambilla, forms the centerpiece to one of the gallery's corridors.*

Three of the National Gallery's most celebrated holdings—Botticelli's "Adoration of the Magi" and Raphael's "St. George and the Dragon" and "The Virgin Mary with the Christ Child and St. John"— entered the collection at that time. The third, called the Alba Madonna after the Duke of Alba, an earlier owner, has the distinction of being the first painting for which a collector was willing to pay more than a million dollars. When Mellon first notified President Roosevelt of his intention to create a national museum, he expressed his hope that the bequest would "attract gifts from other citizens who may in the future desire to contribute works of art ... to form a great national collection." Almost immediately his gesture had just that effect. The Kress Collection of Italian art, including many pre-Renaissance panels, was installed along with Mellon's pictures and sculptures when the National Gallery opened in 1941. Major bequests have since come from Joseph Widener, whose Rembrandts, Vermeers, and El Grecos are among the National Gallery's prizes; from Chester Dale, who contributed major pictures by Monet, Cézanne, Gauguin, Degas, Renoir, Mary Cassatt, George Bellows, and Picasso; from Lessing J. Rosenwald, who provided the prints and drawings department with its core collection; and from scores of other private collectors, including Andrew Mellon's daughter Aisla Mellon Bruce and his son Paul Mellon. Later acquistions have continued to fulfill the original vision of a museum centered on Old Masters—the only picture by Leonardo da Vinci in the western hemisphere, a portrait of Ginevra de Benci, entered the collection in 1967— but the collection's range has expanded to include nineteenth- and twentieth-century art, as well as work by living artists. Special exhibitions are among the major cultural events in Washington each season.

Highlights of the National Gallery's collection include (clockwise, from above) "A Girl with a Watering Can" (1876) by **Auguste Renoir**, "La Mousmé" (1888) by **Vincent van Gogh**, "Four Dancers" (c. 1899) by **Edgar Degas**, "The Death of St. Claire" (c. 1410) by the **Master of Heiligenkreuz**, "Woman with a Parasol—Madame Monet with Her Son" (1875) by **Claude Monet**, and "The Old Musician" (1862) by **Edouard Manet**. The National Gallery owes its existence to the vision, the personal collection and the money of a private citizen, Andrew W. Mellon (1855-1937)

I. M. Pei's design for the National Gallery's **East Building** incorporates **glass pyramids** similar to those he later installed in the courtyard of the Louvre.

Sculptural works commissioned for the East Building include (above) "Orniforme" (1977) after a design by Jean Arp and (below) "Ledge Piece" (1978) by Anthony Caro.

NATIONAL GALLERY OF ART
EAST BUILDING

When the National Gallery of Art opened in 1941 there were, by one person's calculations, 24 works of art to the acre. Whole galleries stood empty. Bequests over the years and an expansion of the gallery's scope to include twentieth-century art resulted, by the 1960s, in an overcrowded building. Andrew Mellon, having foreseen such a need, had reserved a site for expansion as part of the deed donating the original gallery to the nation. The unusual shape of the site (Pennsylvania Avenue's intersection with the other streets forms a trapezoid), its conspicuous location where the Mall meets Capitol Hill, and the neoclassical conservatism of John Russell Pope's original building all presented challenges to the commissioned architect, I. M. Pei. The architect's solution was brilliantly simple: Pei divided the trapezoid into two overlapping triangles, designating one triangle for gallery space and the other for offices, support facilities, and the gallery's large reference library. The new building opened in 1978. Triangles supply the basic unit in Pei's design.

The plaza between the original gallery (the West Building) and the new structure (the East Building) covers an underground connection illuminated by pyramid-shaped skylights anticipating those that Pei later installed in the courtyard of the Louvre. Polygonal towers anchor the building to the site. Huge planes of pink marble (from the same quarry that supplied the West Building) meet at acute angles. As the viewer walks around, the planes seem to shift and move in relationship to each other. At the apex of one of the triangles, to the right of the entrance, the angle where the planes meet is so acute (just 19 degrees) that one of them seems to be as thin as a sheet of paper—a sheet of paper, that is to say, 107 feet high. What the viewer confronts is, in effect, a huge piece of sculpture.

Inside the East Building triangles dictate the shape of the atrium. Even the skylights are defined as concave pyramids. Pei himself has suggested that the source of the building's excitement is the fact that every area, inside and out, possesses not two but

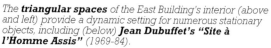

The **triangular spaces** of the East Building's interior (above and left) provide a dynamic setting for numerous stationary objects, including (below) **Jean Dubuffet's "Site à l'Homme Assis"** (1969-84).

An **untitled mobile by Alexander Calder** (above), specially commissioned for the East Building, slowly revolves in the atrium, while (below) **George Segal's "The Dancers"** (1971 and 1982) simulate a turn on the floor.

three axes, not two but three vanishing points. The result, for most visitors, is a sensation of lively movement. The effect is enhanced by a blue and orange 86-foot-long mobile, slowly turning in the atrium's airy openness, which was commissioned from Alexander Calder specifically for this space. A tapestry by Joan Miró, also commissioned as a permanent feature, provides a rich textural contrast to the smoothness of the pink marble walls and floors. Galleries of varied shapes and sizes open off the atrium. The East Building houses most of the National Gallery's collection of modernist and contemporary art, but earlier pictures are also on display. An annual series of special exhibitions fills galleries that were designed just for that purpose. The combination of a varied and changing collection, exhibited in one of the most exciting architectural spaces in the world, makes the East Building one of the most visited museums in America.

*A **sculpted figure of Guardianship** by James Earle Fraser keeps watch over the Constitution Avenue entrance to the National Archives.*

*The building's interior displays original copies of the foundational documents of the American political system, including (below) the **Constitution**.*

NATIONAL ARCHIVES

The original copies of the Declaration of Independence (1776), the Constitution of the United States of America (1787), and the Bill of Rights (1791) are the primary reason that millions of visitors pass each year through the doors of the gigantic mausoleum that John Russell Pope raised in 1935 to house the letters, maps, official documents, diaries, photographs, newspapers, ships' logs, motion pictures, sheet music, microfilms, tape recordings, and assorted emphera produced by the United States government and many of its citizens over the course of two centuries. The Archives' three great treasures are displayed in a monumentally large room, inside cases of protective glass, sealed with inert helium. Every night automatic devices lower the documents into a bombproof vault. It was not until 1952 that the three foundation documents of the American nation were finally united under one roof. More personal reasons draw other visitors to the National Archives. Census records dating back to 1790, military service records, and ship-passenger arrival lists allow amateur genealogists to trace their family history.

Erected in 1911, the **Museum of Natural History** was one of the first buildings in the twentieth-century scheme to realize L'Enfant's original plan for the Mall.

From the **central rotunda** corridors lead off into three domains of knowledge: anthropology, biology, and geology.

NATIONAL MUSEUM OF NATURAL HISTORY
NATIONAL MUSEUM OF MAN

The imperial feeling of the building housing the National Museum of Natural History (completed 1911) is altogether appropriate for a collection that asserts authority over three realms of knowledge—anthropology, biology, and geology—and brings together specimens from all over the world. The museum's collection runs to 121 million items. The largest African bush elephant ever shot, all eight tons of it, greets visitors as they arrive in the museum's 125-foot-high rotunda. Corridors on three floors lead off into the various domains of learning. On the biological front, the museum displays the remains of plants and animals that predate man. They range in size from insects preserved in amber to the bones of Diplodocus, a sauropod dinasaur measuring more than 80 feet from head to tail. Among the fossils on display the oldest is a cabbage-size mass formed by micro-organisms 3.5 billion years ago. Preserved specimens of animals still inhabiting the world today are exhibited in naturalistic settings. North American species like moose, caribou, mountain goats, grizzly bears, and pumas in one area yield place to African animals in another, African animals to Asian animals

in a third. Birds of every climate perch and stare. Visitors are given a rare opportunity to observe penguins close up. Among the fish in the museum's collection is a model of a 92-foot blue whale. To guide them in mounting the preserved specimens, Smithsonian taxidermists began in the 1880s to keep living specimens of some species in pens and cages behind the Castle building. The Smithsonian animals proved so popular with visitors that the zoo was made permanent. In 1889 the live-animal collection—including six bison that had grazed on the Mall—moved to a 163-acre site in Rock Creek Park and became the National Zoo. "Amazonia," a rainforest habitat that is home to free-ranging species, is indicative of the zoo's new self-definition as a BioPark that stresses the natural interdependence of all forms of life. The geology galleries of the Natural History Museum are crammed with stalactites and stalagmites from famous American caverns, every imaginable kind of mineral from around the world, and meteorites from Outer Space. For most visitors, however, the "stars" of the geological collection are the gems. Huge

Life-like displays in the Museum of Natural History turn scientific knowledge into things that visitors can see, hear, and in some cases touch.

*The museum's **collection of fossils** extends back to the beginnings of life in the sea 3.5 billion years ago.*

finished stones like a 138-carat ruby, a 157-carat emerald, a 234-carat topaz, and a 330-carat star sapphire serve as foils for the Hope Diamond, which at 49.5 carats ranks as the largest blue diamond in the world. The third great collecting area, anthropology, has recently become a museum in its own right. Visitors can study skeletal remains and cultural artefacts from all over the globe, including a hand axe from Kenya that is 700,000 years old. Murals and dioramas create a visual context for inserting these objects into the natural environments and social contexts in which they were produced and used. The museum's collection of artefacts is particularly strong on the indigenous peoples of North and South America. Changing special exhibitions focus on particular cultures and assemble artefacts from specialist museums in other parts of the world. At the annual Folklife Festival on the Mall, the Smithsonian brings to Washington representatives of one or more of America's many cultures and ethnic traditions. For a week each July these people tell stories, sing, dance, cook, and practice traditional crafts.

MUSEUM OF AMERICAN HISTORY

The Smithsonian started out as an institute for the study of natural history, conventional enough in the mid-nineteenth century, but in short order it began to accumulate the miscellaneous items that have earned it a description as "the nation's attic." First came the model collection from the U. S. Patent Office. Then Congress deposited all the left-over exhibits from the Philadelphia Centennial Exposition of 1876. The Smithsonian has gone on collecting and never looked back. Assembled under one roof in the Museum of American History (opened 1964) are George Washington's false teeth, Judy Garland's ruby slippers from "The Wizard of Oz," Edison's original light bulb, the largest lump of anthracite coal ever excavated, Henry Ford's Model T, Archie Bunker's chair from the television series "All in the Family," thousands of everyday household objects dating back to colonial times, Frankie Robinson's baseball glove, an authentic stagecoach, linotype

Items in "the nation's attic" include (above) a statue of **Washington in Roman costume** *that graced the Capitol rotunda until it cracked the floor, not to mention the sides of irreverent spectators, and (below)* **monuments to technological development,** *among them a collection of printing presses.*

Boats and ships are among transportation exhibits
that include antique automobiles, steam locomotives,
and a railroad passenger coach dating to 1836.

Re-creations of period interiors give
visitors a context for understanding the uses
of everyday objects from the past.

machines, gunboats from the eighteenth century,
some of the earliest computers—and a seated statue
of a toga-clad George Washington (by Horatio
Greenough, 1840) that there was nowhere else to
put. Several things help make sense of it all. The first
is the dramatic entrance gallery, which displays the
huge shot-torn flag that inspired Francis Scott Key to
write "The Star-Spangled Banner" as a backdrop to
a replica of Léon Foucault's pendulum, a 240-pound
weight suspended on a four-story strand, slowly,
endlessly swinging to mark the earth's rotation.
America against the cycle of time emerges as the
museum's theme. All over the museum
reconstructed room settings provide a context for
the thousands of objects on display. In some of these
settings—an authentic country post office, for
example—visitors can actually walk in and
participate. In the case of a 1910 drug store, they can
even order a soda. The sheer variety of the exhibits
is designed to appeal to the broadest possible range
of visitors. Changing exhibitions allow the museum
to pull down more and more objects out of the attic.

Early morning light casts the **U. S. Capitol** and the base of the **Washington Monument** into high relief.

The Botanic Garden's aluminum and glass conservatories provide ideal environments for plants from all over the world, including a renowned **cactus collection.**

UNITED STATES BOTANIC GARDEN

The stone front of the U. S. Botanic Garden, pretending to be the *orangerie* of a seventeenth-century French chateau, ushers visitors into a gigantic greenhouse made of aluminum and glass. At the time it was built in 1931 it was the largest such structure in the world. Precise climate controls make it possible to provide ideal conditions for plants from all over the globe. Inside the building flourish collections of orchids, begonias, cacti, palms, bromeliads, epiphytes, carnivors, and cycads. Survivors from the age of dinosaurs, cycads produce seeds the size of hen's eggs. Twelve thousand orchids and 313 different types of cactus rank these particular collections among the largest in the world. Several political leaders of the early republic, among them Washington, Jefferson, and Madison, supported the idea of a national botanic garden. The first conservatory was constructed in 1842 to house exotic specimens that explorers brought back from the South Seas. Offspring of some of the original plants are still in the collection. Since 1849 the garden has been located at the eastern end of the Mall. The site it occupies today stands between two beautifully designed natural sites. Eastward stretch the slopes of Capitol Hill, as landscaped in the 1870s by Frederick Law Olmsted, the designer of Central Park in New York City. The west terrace of the Capitol, with its parterres and grand stairways, is Olmsted's creation, as are the monumental lampstands that surround the Capitol grounds. South of the Botanic Garden's greenhouses are geometrically laid out flower beds that provide the setting for a spectacular fountain executed by Frédéric Auguste Bartholdi, designer of the Statue of Liberty, for the 1876 Centennial Exhibition in Philadelphia. Three nymphs in bronze hold up a large basin rimmed with lamps. Electric lights have replaced the gas jets that made the fountain one of the first self-illuminated urban monuments in the world. In addition to Bartholdi Park, the Botanic Garden maintains just west of the conservatory a three-acre demonstration garden in which vegetables and other useful plants are grown each season.

Rockets from America's space exploration program *are gathered in the missile pit of Space Hall, along with the* **Hubble Space Telescope.**

Earlier periods in aviation history are represented by aircraft that includes the original **Wright brothers' "Flyer."**

NATIONAL AIR AND SPACE MUSEUM

Drawing more than ten million visitors a year, the National Air and Space Museum has plausible claims to being the most visited museum in the world. More sight-seers make their way here than to the U. S. Capitol, the Washington Monument, the Lincoln Memorial, and the White House combined. American achievement in flight is the focus of the museum's displays—the building itself opened on July 4, 1976, the two hundredth anniversary of the Declaration of Independence—but the dream of defying mankind's earth-boundedness clearly has an appeal that goes beyond national borders. The building itself manages to catch that dream. Stretching along the Mall for three city blocks, 685 feet, the structure is both monumental and airy at the same time. Alternating bays of pink marble (from the same quarry as the National Gallery of Art across the way) and tinted glass enclose the interior space and yet open it up to views of the Capitol, the other museums up and down the Mall—and the sky.

Twenty-three galleries, covering 200,000 square feet, organize the vast spaces of the building's interior. Gathered in the main hall are planes, rockets, and spacecraft that mark important "Milestones of Flight." Most are originals, not models or copies. The dateline leads from the Wright brothers' "Flyer," which stayed airborne for 59 seconds at Kitty Hawk, North Carolina, in 1903, to the command module "Columbia" that carried astronauts Neil Armstrong, Buzz Aldrin, and Michael Collins to the moon and back in 1969. Highlights along the way include "The Spirit of St. Louis," in which Charles Lindbergh became the first individual to fly nonstop across the Atlantic (1927); the Bell X-1, the first plane to fly beyond the speed of sound (1947); the back-up vehicle for Explorer 1, the first successful American sattelite (1958); "Friendship 7," the Mercury spacecraft in which John Glenn became the first American to orbit the earth (1962); the Gemini IV EVA that carried Edward H. White II for

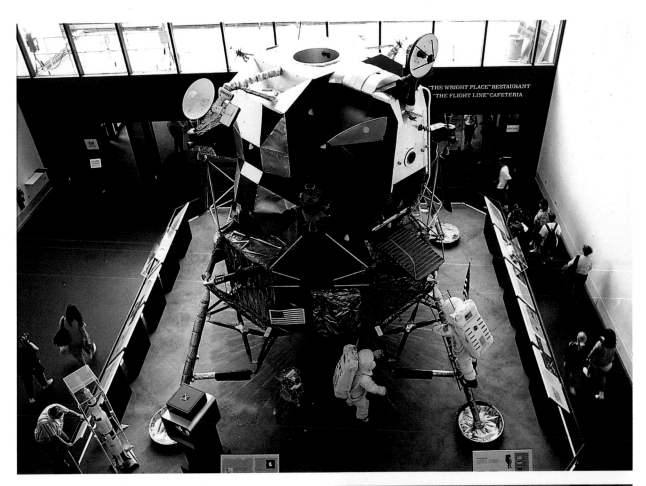

*Vintage **commercial aircraft** (above) and **fighter planes** (below) trace the history of flight in the twentieth century.*

*Spacecraft on display include (above) the **Apollo lunar module**, the backup to the first lunar module flown in orbit.*

the first U.S. walk in space (1965); and the prototype of Pioneer 10, the first spacecraft to explore the outer planets of the solar system. Smaller than any of these exhibits in size but just as large in fascination is a piece of rock from the moon, collected by Apollo 17. Visitors are invited to reach out and touch it. Galleries leading off from the entrance hall explore various aspects of flight. Interactive exhibits on "How Things Fly" start with the basics. The boost given to flight technology by both world wars is apparent in the museum's large collection of vintage aircraft. A gallery called "Where Next, Columbus?" presents some of the challenges that space exploration continues to pose. Two facilities make the solar system and the experience of flight breath-takingly immediate: the Albert Einstein Planetarium, equipped with a Zeiss Model VI projector presented as a Bicentennial gift by the government of Germany, and the Samuel P. Langley Theater, where films on flight and the environment are projected on a screen five stories high and seven stories wide.

Henry Moore's "Two-Piece Reclining Figure: Points" (1969-70) *frames the Hirshhorn Museum's defiantly un-classical frontage on the Mall (above). The Museum's collection of modernist paintings includes (below)* **René Magritte's "Delusions of Grandeur"** *(1948).*

Circular galleries *give visitors a distinctive perspective on twentieth-century art. Two particularly striking focal points are (next page, left)* **Henry Moore's "Falling Warrior"** *(1956-57) and (next page, right)* **Antoine Pevsner's "Column of Peace"** *(1954).*

HIRSHHORN MUSEUM

Art-in-the-round arrived on the Mall in 1974 in the form of the Joseph H. Hirshhorn Museum and Sculpture Garden. Gordon Bunshaft's idiosyncratic building instantly provoked controversy but the art collection that it contains just as quickly established itself as a fixture in Washington's cultural life. Arriving in America from a Latvian ghetto at the age of six, Joseph Hirshhorn was a millionaire several times over by the age of 28. All of his passion and a great deal of his money went into amassing what may be the largest art collection ever assembled by a private individual: 4000 paintings and 2000 pieces of sculpture. In the years just after World War II, when New York was the center of the world market in contemporary art, Hirshhorn was buying on a scale approached by no one else. The result is an accumulation of modern art that has both breadth and depth—two qualities that also distinguish the concrete cylinder that contains the collection. The museum is the site of frequent special exhibitions and an acclaimed film series.

57

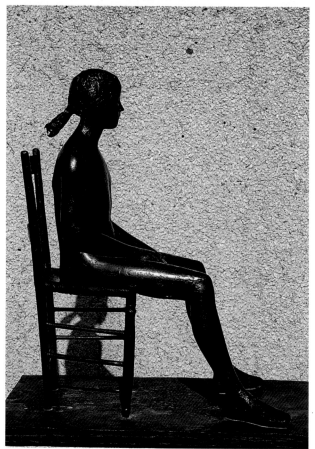

*Sharing space with grass, trees, and sky in the **Hirshhorn Sculpture Garden** are (clockwise from top right) Giacomo Manzu's "Large Standing Cardinal" (1954) and "Young Girl on a Chair" (1955), Auguste Rodin's "Monument to the Burghers of Calais" (1884-89), Marino Marini's "Horse and Rider" (1952-53), and Jean Ipousteguy's "Man Pushing Door" (1966).*

Aristide Maillol's "Action in Chains: Monument to Louis-Auguste Blanqui" (1905-06) illustrates the beginnings of modernism.

HIRSHHORN SCULPTURE GARDEN AND OTHER SMITHSONIAN ART MUSEUMS

In a city where statues typically stand atop pedestals and pediments the Hirshhorn Museum's sculpture garden brings statuary down to a human level. More than 300,000 people each year are enticed to descend from the Mall into a sunken garden laid out with trees, grassy lawns, shrubs, and several dozen pieces of modern sculpture. The garden's two levels invite wandering, small spaces facilitate close-up observation, benches encourage lingering. In date the pieces on display range from the late nineteenth century, when modernism first emerged as a distinct style, to the 1950s and 60s, when Joseph Hirshhorn was most active as a collector. The 1.3-acre Sculpture Garden shows only a part of the museum's huge collection of three-dimensional art. On the plaza beneath the elevated mass of the museum building—itself a piece of sculpture—are Claes Oldenburg's "Geometric Mouse" and Tony Cragg's witty "Subcommittee." Circular galleries inside the museum contain major pieces by Degas, Picasso, and Giacometti, as well as mixed-media installations. Several other specialist art museums are also part of the Smithsonian Institution. The Freer Gallery displays an unusual collection of Asian art and turn-of-the-century American art assembled by Detroit industrialist Charles Lang Freer (1854-1919). The gallery's collection of works by James McNeill Whistler (1834-1903) ranks as the largest and most important in the world.

The Sackler Gallery, founded in 1987 with a group of one thousand Asian masterpieces collected by Arthur M. Sackler, M.D., is not restricted, as the Freer is, to showing only its own holdings. Temporary exhibitions of objects from other Asian art museums and shows of work by living artists make the Sackler a lively center for the study of Asian culture across many centuries and geographic areas. The cultural traditions of the 25 million Americans who trace their ancestry to sub-Saharan Africa find visual expression in the array of objects on display in the Museum of African Art. The permanent collection includes not only the ceremonial masks and figures for which Africa is best known in Europe and America but utilitarian objects that integrate art with everyday life in Africa itself. A museum devoted to Native American culture is scheduled to open early in the twenty-first century.

*In the nineteenth century the picturesque towers of the **Smithsonian Castle building** formed the centerpiece of a Romantic landscape that included groves of trees, wandering paths, and a small herd of bison.*

***James Smithson,** a British aristocrat who never set foot on American soil, looks out over a mall lined with museums that his money helped to found.*

SMITHSONIAN CASTLE

The museums and research institutes that line the Mall—a complex that forms, in effect, America's "National Museum"—owe their existence to someone who never laid foot on American soil in his lifetime. When James Smithson, illegitimate son of the first Duke of Northumberland, died in 1829, he willed his entire estate of £ 104,000 in the first instance to his nephew and, failing an heir, to the United States government "to found at Washington, under the name of the Smithsonian Insitution, an establishment for the increase and diffusion of knowledge among men." Six years later Smithson's nephew died, heirless. It took Congress an astonishing nine years to decide to accept Smithson's bequest, but the result was a research institution devoted primarily to natural history and housed in the red Neo-Gothic prodigy now popularly known as "the Smithsonian Castle." An irregular array of towers and turrets, James Renwick's 1855 structure fitted in perfectly with the meandering paths and picturesque groves that characterized the Mall in the mid nineteenth century. Disinterred from its original resting place in Scotland, Smithson's body shares space today with the administration of the institution his money founded.

Classic marble and monumental bronze take on the **brutal shapes of the concentration camps** *in which millions perished under Nazi rule.*

Artistic responses to the Holocaust *by American schoolchildren (above) line one of the museum's corridors;* **visual documents of camp horrors** *(below) provide a context for hundreds of personal objects left behind by inmates.*

U.S. HOLOCAUST MEMORIAL MUSEUM

In a city full of monuments, the U. S. Holocaust Memorial Museum provokes particularly strong and immediate reactions from visitors. Since its opening in 1993, it has quickly established itself as a major destination. Standing within the shadow of the Washington Monument and commanding a view of the Tidal Basin, the building displays an uneasy relationship with its celebratory environment. On the outside the Holocaust Museum makes superficial gestures of compatibility with its neighborhoods, the red-brick Auditors' Building and the Bureau of Printing and Engraving, but on the inside visitors are confronted at once with the brutal, factory-like functionality that characterized the Nazi-run death camps in which millions of Jews, political dissidents, homosexuals, and others were murdered during the 1930s and 40s. Contrast between the structure's brutality and its human content is striking: on display are clothing, shoes, photographs, personal mementos, and diaries that belonged to individual inmates, along with one of the actual railway cars used to transport Polish Jews to Treblinka.

*At different times of day and night, the **distinctive silhouette of the Washington Monument** turns varying faces of white, gray, gold, and pink to the surrounding city.*

*Ten times taller than its classical exemplars, the Washington Monument (next page) stands as **the tallest masonry structure in the world**.*

WASHINGTON MONUMENT

The cenotaph honoring America's Revolutionary War general and first president remains the tallest masonry structure in the world. At the time it was completed in 1884 it was, indeed, the tallest structure of any kind in the world. At 555 feet 5 inches the Washington Monument is nearly twice as high as the U. S. Capitol, five times higher than any other building in Washington—and ten times higher than any of the Egyptian obelisks that provided models for its design. That such an elegantly simple structure should have such a complicated political history is one of the great ironies of Washington. As early as 1783 the Continental Congress voted to erect a statue of George Washington on horseback wherever the permanent capital came to be. L'Enfant duly provided a location just where the east-west axis from the Capitol crosses the north-south axis from the president's house. When Jefferson tried to place a small marker on the precise spot, the ground proved too boggy to support anything. It was therefore at a higher, drier location 350 feet northeast of L'Enfant's intended spot that work actually began on the monument on July 4, 1848. A private society, founded fifteen years earlier,

provided enough funds to get started and a grandiose plan by Robert Mills, who had designed the monumental column that honors Washington's memory in Baltimore. Difficulties lay ahead. Money problems led to the scrapping of the circular mausoleum Mills had envisioned around the base. Political vandalism (xenophobic "Know-Nothings" first stole an ancient Roman block of stone contributed by Pope Pius IX and then took over the society itself) brought construction to a halt at 156 feet. Then came the Civil War. Cattle for feeding the troops grazed around the base of what Mark Twain called "a factory chimney with the top broken off." When work resumed in 1876 with Congressional support, Mills' design was altered yet again, this time insuring that the finished structure would observe the classical proportions of a height ten times the size of the base. The result is a perfect replica of an ancient obelisk, albeit in a world where people are 60 feet tall. On the inside high-speed elevators and 898 steps take visitors past commemorative stones contributed by numerous foreign countries, many of the states, and a very odd assortment of private societies.

REFLECTING POOL

Stretching nearly 2000 feet from the base of the Lincoln Memorial to the foot of the Washington Monument, the Reflecting Pool helps define one of Washington's grandest vistas. Two miles in the distance looms the dome of the Capitol. In the middle distance rises the magnificent thrust of the Washington Monument. On clear days, visitors to the Lincoln Memorial can look eastward and see the marble mass of the Washington Monument reflected as a shimmering image, disturbed from time to time by swimming ducks and splashing children. Tree-lined avenues down both sides of the pool invite strollers to linger, while jets of water at the Pool's eastern end catch the sunlight and turn it into rainbows. By night, the pool reflects the lighted monument amid the moon and stars. As the pool was nearing completion in the early 1920s, architect Henry Bacon and his friends celebrated by staging a moonlight regatta of flower-trimmed boats. More recent years have seen the launching of a flotilla of hundreds of candles to mark the memory of victims of AIDS.

*Open to the changing sky, the **Reflecting Pool** forms with the Washington Monument a gigantic sundial.*

Architectural forms surrounding the Reflecting Pool *(above) are framed into abstract watercolors.* **Tree-lined walkways** *down both sides of the pool (below) are favorites with walkers, joggers, and cyclists.*

VIETNAM VETERANS MEMORIAL

Flowers, letters, photographs, and personal mementos left behind by visitors give the Vietnam Veterans Memorial an emotional immediacy that is unique in a city full of monuments and memorials. It is the most visited monument on the Mall. It is also the most controversial, just as the war it remembers. When the design competition was won by Maya Ying Lin, a Chinese-American student at Yale University, critics were appalled. Expecting something heroic in white marble, they were confronted instead with a V-shaped black slash in the earth. Where critics found defeatist gloom Lin envisioned regeneration. "Take a knife and cut open the earth," she is quoted as saying, "and with time the grass will heal it." A walk along "the wall" takes the visitor into the dark earth, past the 50,000 etched names of every single American killed in the war, and out again into the light and air.

KOREAN WAR VETERANS MEMORIAL

Documentary realism marks the Korean War Veterans Memorial. Making their way up a slope toward an American flag are 19 soldiers whose service affiliations (15 Army, two Marines, one Navy, one Air Force), race and ethnicity, ages, uniforms, and equipment all represent the historical facts of America's involvement in the Korean War. The soldiers, sculpted by Frank C. Gaylord II, are reflected in a mural wall of polished black granite, etched with hundreds of faces of support personnel—engineers, medics, chaplains, suppliers of matériel—taken from more than 2,500 photographs preserved in the Department of Defense.

The **polished black marble wall** of the Vietnam Memorial (below and right) contains the names of the 50,000 Americans killed in the war.

*Anchoring the western end of the Mall, the Lincoln Memorial stands as a **temple to American ideals.***

LINCOLN MEMORIAL

One of the most familiar icons in American culture (it figures on the back of the five-dollar bill), the Lincoln Memorial performs a series of symbolic functions. It anchors the Mall on its western end, counterbalancing the Capitol at the eastern end. At the same time it commemorates the president whose fate it was to save the union. In doing so, it gives inescapable physical presence to the man and to his words. Daniel Chester French's statue of the seated Lincoln, modeled over a period of thirteen years, is constructed out of twenty separate blocks of Georgia marble, but so skillfully joined together that they give the impression of a single mass. The spirit communicated by that 19-foot-high mass is, however, touchingly human. One of the figure's hands is forcefully clenched; the other, relaxed. The gaze on the face asks to be met and responded to. The martyred president's words take on physical form in huge tablets containing the Gettysburg Address and the Second Inaugural Address. Ornament in a monumental landscape, memorial to a slain president, translation of words and deeds into stone, the Lincoln Memorial also functions as a symbol of civil rights struggles in America. The first event that conferred that symbolic power occurred on Easter Sunday 1939. Refused permission by the Daughters of the American Revolution to sing at Constitution Hall, the great African-American contralto Marian Anderson accepted an invitation from the White House to perform instead from the steps of the Lincoln Memorial. Estimates of the crowd that assembled to hear her range from 30,000 to 75,000. Marian Anderson sang there once again on August 28, 1963, when 250,000 Freedom Marchers gathered at the foot of the memorial to hear Martin Luther King, Jr., utter the simple words "I have a dream ... ." Marchers for women's rights and gay rights have likewise used the Lincoln Memorial as a rallying point. Standing atop reclaimed marshland, the building itself puts the shape and structural elements of a Greek Doric temple to decidedly modern uses. Henry Bacon, the architect, has given access, unusually, from one of temple's broad sides. The 36 columns represent the states of the union at the time of Lincoln's death. On the sides of the Roman-style attic are carved the names of the 48 states at the time of the memorial's completion in 1922.

Foggy Bottom, home to the State Department, looms just beyond the trees in this aerial view of the Lincoln Memorial. Land on which the monument stands was once a marsh.

Henry Bacon's **seated statue of Lincoln** conveys a sense of both power and gentleness.

73

JEFFERSON MEMORIAL

If Thomas Jefferson had won the design competition for the president's house (instead of James Hoban), visitors to the Jefferson Memorial would be able to stand on the steps of this miniature, open-air Pantheon, look across the Tidal Basin, and see in the distance a version of Palladio's domed Villa Rotunda closing the prospect. The vista between the Jefferson Memorial and the White House forms a north-south axis that crosses the east-west axis of the Mall near the Washington Monument. Incumbents in the White House, at least since the Jefferson Memorial was completed in 1943, have looked out the window at a constant reminder of America's polymath third president. Jefferson would have approved of the view. His own design for the new capital featured public walks connecting the major buildings. Fittingly, it was Jefferson's own architectural designs (for the president's house, for the Rotunda Building at the University of Virginia, for his private retreat Monticello) that inspired John Russell Pope's design for the Jefferson Memorial. Rudolph Evans's bronze statue of the president stands amid encircling Ionic columns and four panels with stirring excerpts from Jefferson's speeches and writings. Views of the Jefferson Memorial nestled amid the blossoming cherry trees of the Tidal Basin have emerged as the travel-poster image of Washington, D.C. It is all the more ironic that the spectacle can be enjoyed for only a week to ten days each year (in late March or early April) and that the trees have been the subject of repeated political controversy. The Tidal Basin, having started out as a strictly utilitarian device for flushing the nearby Washington Channel with fresh river water, first acquired its Yoshino cherry trees, a gift from Japan, in 1912, but only after diplomatic embarrassment when the first shipment of trees had to be burned because they were

*Standing amid cherry trees in Potomac Park, along one side of the **Tidal Basin,** the Jefferson Memorial forms one of the most famous icons of Washington.*

infested with insect pests and fungus diseases. After the Japanese attack on Pearl Harbor in 1941, vandals destroyed several of the trees. When trees were being removed to make way for the Jefferson Memorial, angry protestors plopped themselves down into the holes that were left and chained themselves to the survivors. A happier political event was the shipping of cuttings to Japan in 1952 to replace some of the parent trees.

*The Jefferson Memorial incorporates **Roman architectural elements**—in particular the circular design of the Pantheon—that Jefferson favored in his own building plans.*

*__Ionic columns__ (below) encircle Rudolph Evans's **bronze statue of President Jefferson** (right), wearing a greatcoat supposed to have been given to him by the Polish patriot Thadeus Kosciuszko.*

The **north portico** (above) forms the ceremonial entrance to the White House. **Andrew Jackson** (below) in his guise as hero of the War of 1812 tips his hat as he rides past the building he occupied as president from 1829 to 1837.

The south portico of the White House (above) incorporates a homey balcony added by President Harry Truman. The south lawn (next page) is the scene of parties and receptions, as well as the president's arrivals and departures by helicopter.

THE WHITE HOUSE

Television news broadcasts have made The White House one of the most recognized images in the world. Having first seen it close up on a television screen, many first-time visitors are struck by the modest size of what is, after all, an eighteenth-century country house enveloped by a huge city. The surroundings were altogether different when Abigail Adams moved in with her husband John, the second president, in 1800. "The country round is romantic," she wrote to her sister, "but a wild wilderness at present." Under construction since 1792, the building still was not finished when the Adamses arrived, and Mrs. Adams used the East Room for hanging out the laundry. Jefferson, the next occupant, found the place "big enough for two

emperors, one Pope, and the grand Lama." His own design for the building, submitted anonymously, had been passed over in favor of one by James Hoban, an Irish-American who was a self-taught architect. To offset the pompous effect, Jefferson added two low-lying terrace-pavilions that are still used for offices and service functions. Succeeding occupants have left their own marks on the place, notably Harry Truman, who upset purists by adding a balcony to the curved South Portico, and Jacqueline Kennedy, who cleared out a century and a half of accumulated furnishings and restored the public rooms to something like their early nineteenth-century appearance. The most disastrous moment in White House history came in August 1814, when the British

*Situated within the curved south walls of the White House, the **Blue Room** (above) contains furniture from the time of President James Monroe. The **Red Room** (below), used today as a sitting room, once was the waiting room for callers wishing to see the President, whose library was next door.*

*The **Oval Office,** situated in an extension of one of the terraces added by Jefferson, has been the workplace of every president since William Howard Taft in 1909.*

invaded Washington and set the building afire. Dolly Madison, left alone to hold the house, managed to get out just in time, first sending away "the plate and most valuable portable articles belonging to the house," as well as Gilbert Stuart's full-length portrait of George Washington, which still dominates the East Room. A violent summer thunderstorm saved the house from total destruction. Hoban's reconstruction of the building over the next four years included a coat of white wash, perhaps to hide scorch marks from the British flames. The name "White House," in use from the very beginning to describe the structure's creamy sandstone, did not become official until 1902.

*Clark Mills's **statue of Andrew Jackson** (above), erected in 1853, was the first equestrian statue to be designed and cast by an American. The **Blair and Lee Houses** (below) are two of many elegant townhouses that surround Lafayette Square.*

*A 15-foot gilt statue of Winged Victory, by Daniel Chester French, crowns the World War I **First Division Memorial**, south of the Old Executive Office Building. The nearby **Octagon House** anticipates I. M. Pei's East Building in finding an elegant solution to an awkward site.*

LAFAYETTE SQUARE

Lafayette Square became a square when Thomas Jefferson, objecting to imperial pretense, detached it from the grounds of the White House. It became Lafayette Square in 1824 when the Revolutionary War hero was feted there. By the mid-nineteenth century it had become a fashionable address, as witness the elegant townhouses that surround it on three sides. Andrew Jackson, hero of the Battle of New Orleans (1814), rides proud in the center. Revolutionary War heroes hold down the corners. They are accompanied most days by protestors and demonstrators.

BLAIR HOUSE

Two once separate houses have been joined together to form guest quarters for visiting dignitaries and heads-of-state. The original Blair House, built in 1824, acquired its name when it was purchased in 1837 by Francis P. Blair, friend of Andrew Jackson and founder of the pro-Jackson *Washington Globe*. The house next door was built in 1859 by Admiral Phillips Lee as a gift to his bride Elizabeth, daughter of Francis Blair. While the White House was being renovated during the 1950s Blair House provided temporary quarters for President Harry Truman and his family.

OLD EXECUTIVE OFFICE BUILDING

Flaunting its Second Empire eclecticism, the Old Executive Office Building (1875-1888) seems to affront everything around it; in particular, the sober Treasury Building, which occupies a symmetrical place on the other side of the White House. "The ugliest building in America," as Mark Twain is supposed to have called it, nonetheless witnessed the signing of thousands of treaties while the State Department was in residence. The departments of War and the Navy were also quartered here until they decamped for the Pentagon. Among the tenants today are the offices of the Vice President.

THE OCTAGON HOUSE

Commissioned by Colonel James Tayloe III, a Virginia gentlemen who was a graduate of Eton and Christ Church, Cambridge, the Octagon House (c. 1800) was designed by William Thornton, the amateur architect who earlier had won the competition for the Capitol's design. Spared burning by the British during the War of 1812, it became the temporary White House for James and Dolley Madison and the site of the treaty-signing that ended the war. The American Institute of Architects owns the property today.

CORCORAN GALLERY OF ART

Pre-dating all of America's major art museums, the Corcoran was established in 1859 "for the encouragement of American genius." William Wilson Corcoran pursued that aim by opening up his collection of paintings, sculpture, and casts to the public and by founding an art school that continues to this day. American art is the focus of the permanent collection. A biennial exhibition showcases contemporary painting.

AMERICAN NATIONAL RED CROSS

Built on public land with both public and private funds, the headquarters of the American Red Cross typifies the organization's partly official, partly private status. When it was erected in 1913-17, the building was conceived as a memorial "to the heroic women of the Civil War." Chief among them was Clara Barton, the founder of the Red Cross, who ministered to the wounded in public buildings throughout the city.

CONSTITUTION HALL

Violinist Efrem Zimbalist inaugurated what for many years was Washington's only major concert hall. With a capacity of 4000, it remains Washington's largest. John Russell Pope's edifice, built to house conventions of the Daughters of the American Revolution, was completed in 1929. The DAR's refusal of the hall to Marian Anderson in 1939 occasioned the African-American contralto's outdoor recital at the Lincoln Memorial.

ORGANIZATION OF AMERICAN STATES

The world's oldest international organization—a federation of the nations of North, South, and Central America established in 1890—is housed in a white marble building that brings together stylistic elements of many cultures. Within a Beaux Arts frame are to be found a tropical patio built around a fountain that combines Mayan, Aztec, and Zapotecan motifs; Aztec gardens; and a gallery devoted to contemporary art.

EINSTEIN MEMORIAL

On the grounds of the National Academy of Sciences stands a monument to a scientist who taught the world to think of space and time as space-time. Robert Berk's informal bronze likeness of Einstein, three times life size, lolls on a stone bench. At his feet is a circular sky map laid out on a 28-foot expanse of pearl granite. More than 2,700 metal studs represent the sun, moon, stars, and planets.

*The classical facades of the **Corcoran Gallery**, the American **Red Cross**, and **Constitution Hall**, all of them along 17th Street, N.W., compose one of Washington's noblest vistas.*

*The **Organization of American States** (above) occupies a building that, like the organization itself, combines several distinct cultures. **Albert Einstein** (below) casts a relativistic eye on visitors to grounds of the National Academy of Sciences.*

*James Earle Fraser's statue of **Alexander Hamilton,** first Secretary of the Treasury (1789-95), presides over the south entrance plaza to the Treasury Building.*

*The stretch of **Pennsylvania Avenue** from the Capitol to the White House (above) contains a microcosm of Washington architecture, from small mid-nineteenth-century commercial buildings to bureaucratic prodigies like the **FBI Building** (below).*

TREASURY BUILDING

Andrew Jackson is supposed to have said *"Here* is where I want the cornerstone," and *there* the Treasury Building is—blocking L'Enfant's planned vista between the White House and Capitol. Jackson was impatient with political squabbling about where the new building should be. Both of its predecessors had burned. Jackson walked out of the White House one morning (so the story goes), planted his cane in the ground, made his declaration, and that was that. The vista may be gone, but the stately Greek Revival building that arose in its place is one of Washington's best known landmarks. (It figures on the back of the ten-dollar bill.) Robert Mills contributed the original design and survived political skirmishes long enough to complete the middle portion of the east range. The rest of the project was carried out between 1836 and 1869 by a succession of other architects. Recent restoration to the interior has returned spaces like the two-story Cash Room to their original splendor.

PENNSYLVANIA AVENUE

Stretching from the Capitol to the White House, "America's Main Street" has provided the route for countless presidential inaugural parades, protest marches, victory celebrations, and funeral processions. The regimented edifices of the Federal Triangle line the south side of the avenue; buildings forming a virtual catalogue of nineteenth- and twentieth-century styles jut in and out on the north side.

FBI

No secrecy here. The headquarters of the Federal Bureau of Investigation asserts its presence in a huge fortress-like building erected amid great public controversy in 1974. Designed by Stanley Gladych in the idiom of Le Corbusier's "International Style," the structure plays on a contrast between heavy concrete building material and airy weightlessness. Blocks of offices are suspended between tower-like pylons.

*Inside and out, the idiosyncratic **Old Post Office Building** offers welcome relief from the neo-classical regularities of official Washington.*

*The **Navy Memorial** occupies an open space along Pennsylvania Avenue that was once a bustling produce market.*

OLD POST OFFICE BUILDING

Neoclassical conformists hate it; admirers of the odd and the eccentric love it. Amid the Roman regularities of the Federal Triangle, the Old Post Office Building (1899) refuses to be awed. Its clock tower (with hands 5.5 and 7.5 feet long) rises high above its neighbors and insinuates itself into the view anywhere a stroller happens to be along Pennsylvania Avenue. The fortress-like Romanesque exterior covers one of the first steel constructions in the city—and an airy atrium covered by an immense roof of glass. Continually threatened with demolition since the Post Office moved out in 1934, the building proved too big and too expensive to demolish through the 1930s and 40s. In 1983 rescue came in the form of a complete rehabilitation to multiple public uses. Today, office workers and school groups throng the atrium's food court and sight-seers ride the open-cage elevator to the clock tower, while officials of the National Endowments for the Arts and the Humanities work away in upstairs offices.

MARKET SQUARE

Now the site of two *neo*-neoclassical buildings erected in 1990, Market Square was indeed a vegetable and meat market until the City Beautiful movement banished such functions to less prominent locations during the first decade of the twentieth century. Earlier visitors describe a lively scene at this location, as boarding-house keepers thronged the stalls to do their daily shopping. Today's visitors will find a pair of monumental colonnades embracing a semicircular space in which a brace of masts and a lone bronze figure keep watch as the Navy Memorial. The Market Square development, which houses shops, offices, restaurants, and condominiums, fits in well with its neoclassical neighbors across Pennsylvania Avenue at the same time that it contributes to the liveliness of the nearby Seventh Street art and theater district. The buildings' curves also help to define two of Washington's great vistas, up the avenue toward the Capitol and up Eighth Street from the National Archives to the National Portrait Gallery.

*Ford's Theater, the **scene of President Lincoln's assassination** in 1865, has been restored as both a memorial and a working theater.*

*Period furnishings, including pieces original to the house, make the **Petersen House** feel much as it did on April 15, 1865, when the wounded Lincoln died in a **small back bedroom** (below).*

FORD'S THEATER

The date was April 14, 1865. The Civil War had ended five days before, when Robert E. Lee had surrendered to Ulysses S. Grant at Appomattox, Virginia. At John T. Ford's two-year-old theater on Tenth Street Tom Taylor's comedy *Our American Cousin* was slated for its final night, with the celebrated actress Laura Keene in one of the main roles. President Lincoln, an admirer of Miss Keene, was advertised on playbills as planning to attend. Also in attendance that night was John Wilkes Booth, an actor whose performances Lincoln had twice enjoyed at Ford's Theater. Near the beginning of the second act Booth, who was well known to the theater management, gained access to the president's box and, taking advantage of the audience's laughter at a funny line, fired a shot point-blank into Lincoln's scull. He leapt to the stage to announce his vengence on behalf of the Confederacy and escaped into the night. The president died the next morning. Restored as closely as possible to its appearance on the fateful night, Ford's Theater once again operates as a working theater. A small museum displays the murder weapon, the boots Lincoln wore to the theater, and other artefacts.

THE PETERSEN HOUSE

In a small back bedroom of this brick row house President Abraham Lincoln died early in the morning of April 15, 1865. He had been mortally wounded the night before at Ford's Theater across the street. Doctors advised against taking the unconscious president back to the White House over rough cobbled streets. Suddenly cast as the scene of a public tragedy, the little house had been built in 1849 by William Petersen, a Swedish immigrant who worked as a tailor on the first floor and rented out rooms to lodgers. The back bedroom belonged to his daughter Pauline, who was away at boarding school.
When restoration began on the house in the 1920s Pauline Petersen Wenzing was able to give precise information about the room's furnishings. Visitors to the site today can see the parlor in which Mrs. Lincoln waited, the room in which the secretary of war carried out his investigation of the crime, and the bedroom in which Lincoln died. The bed itself is a reproduction, but on it lies one of the bloodied pillows that cushioned the president's head.

*The **National Portrait Gallery** and the **Museum of American Art** occupy premises that have served as the capital's first art museum, a conservatory for exotic plants, a Civil War hospital, a museum of patented inventions, and the site of presidential balls.*

*The monumental exterior of the **National Building Museum**.*

DOWNTOWN

NATIONAL PORTRAIT GALLERY

A monument to Greek sobriety in a city of Roman excess, the complex of buildings that house the National Portrait Gallery and the Museum of American Art occupies a site that L'Enfant reserved for a "shrine to American heroes." The Portrait Gallery serves that function today, but only after the buildings housed the Patent Office, a Civil War hospital, and the Civil Service Commission. Begun in 1836 according to the solid, fire-proof designs of Robert Mills, the buildings were the largest in the entire country when they were completed in 1867—the nineteenth-century equivalent of the Pentagon. The colonnaded Lincoln Gallery encapsulates the buildings' history. Walt Whitman saw the gallery decked out for Lincoln's second inaugural ball in 1865, just months after he had helped Clara Barton, founder of the Red Cross, tend mortally wounded soldiers in the same room. Today the gallery houses modernist paintings from the collection of the Museum of American Art, which started out as the National Institute, in this very building, in 1841.

NATIONAL BUILDING MUSEUM

The National Building Museum stands as testimony to how one era's white elephant can become another era's architectural treasure. Having helped to engineer the Capitol's new dome during the Civil War, Montgomery C. Meigs, quartermaster general of the Union Army, was asked after the war to design a building for distributing military pensions. This gargantuan red-brick version of Michelangelo's Palazzo Farnese was the result. Inside is to be found one of Washington's truly stupendous spaces, a colonnaded atrium 316 feet long, 116 feet wide, and 159 feet high. A huge clerestory admits enough light to keep the interior bright in winter and enough air to keep it cool in summer. The Corinthian columns carrying the roof, 15 feet taller than the colossal columns at Baalbek, may be the largest Roman columns ever constructed. Recently restored after a century of critical abuse and physical neglect, the structure now houses the National Building Museum, dedicated to an appreciation of all kinds of buildings, in all kinds of circumstances.

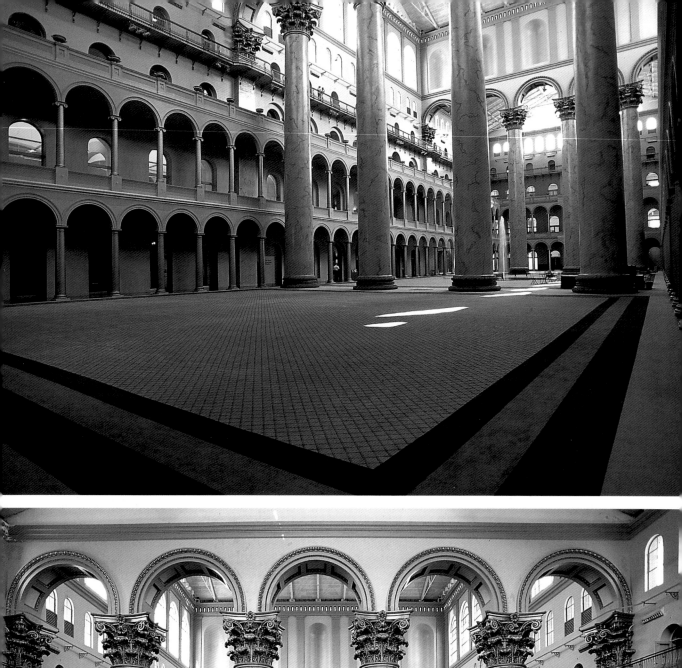

*Distant memories of ancient Rome and Michelangelo haunt the interior of the **National Building Museum.***

*Daniel Chester French's **maritime memorial to Rear Admiral Samuel F. Dupont**, with statues of Sea, Stars, and Wind, forms the centerpiece to one of Washington's most vibrant neighborhoods.*

DUPONT CIRCLE

For the newly rich self-made men of late nineteenth-century America there were two prime places for building a mansion, setting up the family, and cutting a figure in society: Fifth Avenue in New York City and Dupont Circle in Washington. Personal income tax and the Great Depression put an end to the economy that made such a life possible, but a rich architectural legacy remains in the form of grand houses that now quarter embassies, social clubs, and professional associations. It was a group of speculators, the so-called California Syndicate, who developed the area around "Pacific Circle" in the 1870s. The name was changed in 1882 to honor Samuel Francis duPont, Civil War naval hero and scion of a Delaware family whose old wealth gave a patina to the new money in the neighborhood. It was the duPont family themselves who in the 1920s commissioned Daniel Chester French, sculptor of the Lincoln Memorial, to make the marble fountain that forms the centerpiece for one of Washington's most cosmopolitan neighborhoods.

PHILLIPS COLLECTION

The first gallery of modern art in America still feels like a private home. Small rooms invite intimate viewing. Sofas and chairs provide places to sit down. Sunday afternoon concerts in the music room send music drifting all over the house. The Phillips Collection, opened to the public in 1921, was indeed the private home of the collectors, Duncan and Marjorie Phillips—though not for long. Their generosity soon forced them to move to new quarters. The house itself had been built by Duncan Phillips's father in 1897. The personal taste of the collectors distinguishes the paintings on view. Giorgione, El Greco, Goya, Daumier, Thomas Eakins, and Winslow Homer share space with the artists for which the collection is noted: Van Gogh, Monet, Bonnard, Gauguin, Klee, Braque, Picasso, Mark Rothko, and Georgia O'Keefe. Most famous of all, perhaps, is Renoir's "The Boating Party." The public to whom the Phillipses introduced these modern artists included future members of the Washington Colorist School.

*A variety of period styles make **the mansions of Embassy Row** an architectural tour-de-force.*

*Civil War General **Philip H. Sheriden** holds down one of Embassy Row's strategic positions.*

EMBASSY ROW

Partly a legacy of Gilded Age extravagence, partly a showcase of modern and post-modern design, Embassy Row stretches along Massachusetts Avenue, N.W., from Dupont Circle to Washington National Cathedral. Many of the buildings that today house foreign legations, especially toward the Dupont Circle end, were built as private residences between 1880 and 1910. Their owners were tycoons who had made their money elsewhere but were taking up residence in Washington to give their wealth an aura of gentility and to gain handy access to the corridors of power. Mansions that looked like French châteaux, Palladian palazzi, and Mayfair townhouses served their purposes nicely. Notable examples are the embassies of Indonesia at 2020 Massachusetts Avenue (Walsh-McLean House, 1903), Haiti at 2311 (Fahrtestock House, 1909), Pakistan at 2315 (Moran House, 1908), Cameroon at 2349 (Hauge House, 1906), and Turkey at 1606 23rd Street (Everett House, 1914). Farther up the avenue are a series of purpose-built embassies that exemplify various schools of twentieth-century architectural design, including Sir Edwin Lutyens' wittily allusive British Embassy (1927-28) at 3100,

Delano and Aldrich's cross-cultural Japanese Embassy (1931) at 2520, Olavo de Campo's suave modernist chancery for the Brazilian Embassy (1973) at 3000, and Mikko Heikkinen and Markku Komonen's startling post-modern Finnish Embassy (1994) at 3301. Part way along Massachusetts Avenue is Sheridan Circle, centered on a statue of Civil War hero General Philip H. Sheriden by Gutzon Borglum, whose most famous piece of sculpture is one of the largest works ever attempted by man: the colossal likenesses of Presidents Washington, Jefferson, Lincoln, and Theodore Roosevelt on Mount Rushmore in South Dakota. Teddy Roosevelt himself was on hand for the dedication of General Sheriden's statue in 1909. In a street of cultural eclecticism the most exotic note of all is struck by the Islamic Center at number 2551. Constructed by the Egyptian Ministry of Works in 1949 as a religious center for all American Moslems, the building is oriented to face Mecca and contains a brilliant array of faience tile, carpets, wood inlay work, and stained glass. Two other embassies of architectural note are those of Germany (1964) and France (1985), both located on Reservoir Road northwest of Georgetown.

Commanding a prospect over the city from Mount St. Alban, **Washington National Cathedral** was under construction for most of the twentieth century.

Every detail of the cathedral's **interior** was carried out by craftsmen using medieval techniques.

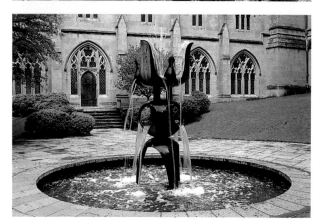

WASHINGTON NATIONAL CATHEDRAL

L'Enfant's vision of a "great church for national purpose ... equally open to all" has been realized only in the twentieth century with the construction of the Washington National Cathedral. Begun in 1907, the building was finished in 1990. Although erected under auspices of the Protestant Episcopal Church, the cathedral defines its mission as ecumenical. Funerals and memorial services for many national heroes have been held there. Chapels within the cathedral have provided parish homes for Polish, Russo-Carpathian, Syrian, and Serbian Orthodox churches. Martin Luther King, Jr., preached his last Sunday sermon from the cathedral's pulpit. Only a single vote prevented the cathedral from being built in the neoclassical style of most of Washington's public buildings. Constructed in the idiom of fourteenth-century English Gothic, using medieval building techniques, Washington National Cathedral may well be the last great Gothic building to be attempted anywhere in the world.

*This aerial view shows how Georgetown, even today, remains a **self-contained town** within the city of Washington.*

*Lined with warehouses and factories that have been converted to stylish uses, the **Chesapeake and Ohio Canal** was once Georgetown's link to the wild west.*

GEORGETOWN

C&O CANAL

Retaining today its own social identity and architectural distinction, Georgetown was an established community within the state of Maryland two generations before the District of Columbia and the City of Washington were ever envisioned. It was at a gathering in Mayor Uriah Forrest's townhouse, still standing at 3350 M Street, N.W., that local landowners were persuaded by George Washington to sell to the federal government the tracts needed for laying out the new capital to the east of town. The "George" in Georgetown was not George Washington but King George II (reigned 1727-1760), father of the king who received the Declaration of Independence. As settlers pressed westward into Virginia, Maryland, and the frontier beyond, Georgetown stood to expand its shipping trade—but for one obstacle: the Great Falls of the Potomac just upriver. At the close of the Revolutionary War, George Washington was one of several investors in a project to build a canal detour around the falls.

Substantial remains of the canal still can be seen in Great Falls Park, Virginia. In 1828 a more ambitious project was begun, to build a canal all the way from Georgetown to Ohio. By the time the first 185 miles had been completed, the railroad had already beat the Chesapeake and Ohio Canal to its western markets. Georgetown then settled into genteel obsolesence while the brash new federal city all around it grew by leaps and bounds. In 1871 Georgetown lost its charter and self-government, officially becoming part of the City of Washington for the first time. The port's once important Customs House (1857) became a branch post office; even the street names were changed to accord with those of the rest of the city. Commercial activity along the C&O Canal continued until the 1920s, but it was a new generation of residents, drawn to the area's colonial atmosphere, that began in the 1940s and 50s to transform Georgetown into the stylish part of town it remains today. Warehouses and mills along the C&O canal have recently been converted into offices, shops, art galleries, restaurants, and condominiums.

OLD STONE HOUSE

Washington's oldest surviving building, the Old Stone House in Georgetown was built about 1766 by Christopher Layman, who lived in the house and ran a cabinet-making shop there. At the time, Georgetown had been established for only fifteen years or so. Major land grants in the area date to 1703, when Ninian Beall obtained a patent for The Rock of Dumbarton. George Gordon soon established Rock Creek Plantation nearby. Other settlers, many of them Scots like Beall and Gordon, arrived over the next forty years. Export of tobacco from up-country plantations and import of household goods and rum provided the reason for the port city's establishment in 1751. At the time Georgetown stood on the western frontier of colonial civilization. The humble proportions and rough-hewn functionality of the Old Stone House help explain why Abigail Adams, moving into the still unfinished White House in 1800, could exclaim, "Such a place as Georgetown! ... It is the very dirtyest Hole I ever saw for a place of any trade or respectability of inhabitants." The great federal houses that distinguish Georgetown today were, in 1766, still more than thirty years in the future.

*Simple in design and sturdy in construction, the Old Stone House (above) is **Washington's oldest surviving building.** The interior (below) is as spare as the exterior.*

*Tools and planks give some idea of how the Old Stone House functioned as a **cabinet-maker's shop** (above). The Layman family's **living quarters** (below) are evocative of daily life on what, in 1766, was America's western frontier.*

The dominant feel of Georgetown comes from houses constructed in the early years of the federal republic, like **"Cox's Row"** along what once was called First Street.

Eighteenth- and early nineteenth-century mansions line the heights above Georgetown. **Dumbarton House** is the oldest.

FEDERAL HOUSES

The 3300 block of N Street, N.W., (formerly First Street) typifies the federal architecture that abounds in Georgetown. Geometrical simplicity and plainness of detail distinguish the federal houses of Georgetown from their more ornamented Georgian counterparts in Old Town Alexandria down the river. "Cox's Row," as the 3300 block is called, was built between 1815 and 1818 by John Cox, a merchant who served as mayor of Georgetown for 22 years. When in 1824-25 the Marquis de Lafayette payed his last visit to the country he had helped to liberate, Cox offered the house that is now number 3337 as a temporary residence. Lafayette accepted the offer. In social scale the townhouses of Cox's Row were midway between great estates like Dumbarton House and the humbler houses of workers and artisans. Until the 1960s Georgetown was home to an economically diverse population, including a substantial African-American community. Mount Zion United Methodist Church, thought to be the oldest African-American congregation in Washington, traces its history back to 1816 and still holds services in a late nineteenth-century building at 1334 29th Street, N.W., on Georgetown's eastern side.

DUMBARTON HOUSE

Dating to about 1798, Dumbarton House is probably the oldest of the great houses that crown the heights above Georgetown.
The others are Evermay (1801), Dumbarton Oaks (1801), the Bowie-Sevier House (1805), and Tudor Place (1816).
Dumbarton, like most of the others, was originally connected with a great tract of land.
The first owner of the site was Ninian Beall, who in 1703 secured a patent for 705 acres which he called "The Rock of Dumbarton," after the castle along the River Clyde in his Scottish homeland. The tract included much of the land on which Georgetown stands today. The extant house was designed and built by its first owner, Samuel Johnson. When Joseph Nourse, holder of important positions under Washington, Jefferson, and Madison, acquired the property about 1805, he ordered important alterations to be carried out by Benjamin Henry Latrobe, one of the architects of the original U. S. Capitol.
Dumbarton House serves today as headquarters of the National Society of the Colonial Dames of America.

Commerce has always been the reason for Georgetown's existence. The enclosed spaces of **Georgetown Park** (above) have joined **small shops in older structures** (below) to ensure Georgetown's contemporary reputation as a stylish shopping destination.

A **trompe-l'oeil** evocation of eighteenth-century Georgetown (above) joins **the real thing** (below) to give the neighborhood its antique charm.

GEORGETOWN PARK

The feed stores, automobile repair shops, pharmacies, and hardware stores that once served Georgetown as a working community have given way for the most part to art galleries, antique stores, bars, restaurants, coffee houses, clothing boutiques, upscale food markets, and bookstores. A relic of the old days survives in Stohlman's Confectionary Shop (founded 1854), the interior of which was removed in 1957 from a building still standing at 1254 Wisconsin Avenue and is now reconstructed inside the Museum of American History on the Mall. Examples of the new wave of shops are concentrated in Georgetown Park, a 1980s development that incorporates several older buildings into a sprawling, multi-storied shopping mall with skylights, tile floors, and cast-iron fittings that recall the shopping galleries of nineteenth-century European cities. Among the historic structures that adjoin Georgetown Park are an early nineteenth-century firehouse and one of Washington's original public food markets.

KEY BRIDGE

The magnificent arches of Key Bridge have spanned the Potomac River at one of its most scenic reaches since 1923. The bridge takes its name from Francis Scott Key's mansion, which stood nearby. It was from this house that Key departed by boat on September 12, 1814, and made his way by water to Baltimore, to rescue a friend who had been captured by the British. While anchored in Baltimore harbor, Key witnessed the British bombardment of the city and was inspired to write "The Star-Spangled Banner."

WASHINGTON HARBOUR

Outdated industrial buildings along Georgetown's waterfront yielded place in 1986 to a huge complex of shops, restaurants, offices, and condominiums. Washington Harbour, designed by Arthur Cotton Moore, has had the happy effect of opening up some of Georgetown's streets to the river. From the promenade there are broad views across to the wooded shores of Roosevelt Island and down river to the Kennedy Center. On warm weekends pleasure boats anchor at the dock, diners enjoy open-air restaurants, and strollers take the air.

GEORGETOWN UNIVERSITY

History, academic reputation, a renowned basketball team, famous alumni, and a scenic campus draw visitors to the gates of Georgetown University.

The oldest Catholic institution of higher learning in the United States, the university traces its history to an academy founded in 1789.

Charles Dickens, visiting the hilltop at the western edge of Georgetown in 1842, found pleasant things to say about the place. He noted the ecumenical character of the institution and was inspired to observe that "The heights in this neighborhood, above the Potomac River, are very picturesque."

The towered Healy Building (1879), named for Patrick Healy, a partly African-American Jesuit priest who served as president of the university in the nineteenth century, dominates the campus and the view from the Potomac.

Behind the granite facade are to be found federalist red-brick reminders of the university's more distant past, particularly Old North Hall (1792-93), from the steps of which George Washington addressed the student body. More than 10,000 students attend the university today.

Georgetown's historic connection to the Potomac River is affirmed by **Key Bridge** *(above) and the* **Washington Harbour development** *(below).*

The oldest Catholic institution of higher learning in the United States, **Georgetown University** *boasts a spectacular location, a high academic reputation, and a famed basketball team.*

The **Watergate Complex** (left) and the **Kennedy Center**
(right) front the Potomac River in Foggy Bottom.

The nine arches of **Memorial Bridge** (above) link the
Mall with Arlington National Cemetery in Virginia.
Statues of the Arts of War and the Arts of Peace
(below) flank the Washington end of the bridge.

KENNEDY CENTER AND WATERGATE

Vast public spaces, six performance venues, and a
performing arts library make up a living memorial
to John F. Kennedy. Although a cultural center for the
nation's capital had been discussed since the 1930s, it
took the assassination of an arts-minded president to
get one built. Edward Durrell Stone's modernist
restatement of the Lincoln Memorial, situated just
down the river, opened in 1971. The grand foyer,
630 feet long and six stories high, is dominated by a
huge bust of Kennedy by Robert Berks. Gifts from
many nations enrich the center's interior.

Unlike many real-estate ventures in America, the
Italian-designed Watergate Complex is named for a
real place. Just down the river, where Arlington
Memorial Bridge crosses Rock Creek Parkway, a
huge arc of steps leads down from the Lincoln
Memorial to the shores of the Potomac. This original
Watergate, built in 1931, was designed to receive
important visitors who might arrive by water. The
steps' 1971 namesake is one of Washington's most
prestigious addresses as well as the site of political
espionage that cost Richard Nixon his job as president.

ARLINGTON

ARLINGTON MEMORIAL BRIDGE

According to Charles Moore, secretary to the
McMillan Commission, it was a vista in the
gardens of the Villa Borghese in Rome that inspired
the commissioners to envision a low monumental
bridge connecting the Lincoln Memorial with
Arlington National Cemetery. It was a colossal traffic
jam that got the bridge built. On Armistice Day 1921
a ceremonial motorcade bound for Arlington
Cemetery got stuck for two hours trying to cross the

Fourteenth Street Bridge and negotiate back roads
from the bridge to the cemetery. Funding for the
long-foreseen Memorial Bridge was soon
forthcoming. The elegant nine-arched span was
completed in 1932. Heroic statues of The Arts of
War, by Leo Friedlander, and The Arts of Peace, by
James Earle Fraser, anchor the Washington end of
the bridge. Although designed in the 1920s, the
statues were not erected until 1951, after the Italian
government offered to cast and gild the statues as a
symbol of friendship between Italy and America.

The most recent addition to the **grave site of John F. Kennedy** in Arlington Cemetery is the grave (right) of Jacqueline Kennedy Onassis.

The **Tomb of the Unknown Soldier** (above) is the most prominent among more than 200,000 graves that fill Arlington Cemetery's 420 acres.

ARLINGTON NATIONAL CEMETERY

The Doric portico of Arlington House (built 1803-1818), a plantation house associated with the families of both George Washington and Robert E. Lee, commands two unrivaled views: one over the City of Washington and another over two centuries of American history in the form of 200,000 graves that fill Arlington National Cemetery. Slave labor built the mansion and worked the estate that was inhabited by George Washington Parke Custis, adopted son of George Washington. Robert E. Lee took possession of the plantation when he married Custis's only surviving child, Mary Ann Randolph Custis, in 1831. It was in his study in Arlington House, on April 20, 1861, that Lee drafted the letter in which he resigned his commission in the U. S. Army and proclaimed his loyalties to Virginia. When the Union Army arrived to claim the site as a fortress, the Lee family fled, losing the property three years later after failing to pay U. S. taxes that had to be tendered in person. By then,

Robert E. Lee was commander of the rebel army. The Arlington estate first became a cemetery while it was being used as a military camp. The first person to be buried, as it happened, was a Confederate soldier who had died in captivity. By the war's end nearly 5000 people had been interred in the original plot's 210 acres. Of these, 3802 are African-Americans who had fled slavery by attaching themselves to the Union Army. Military burials continued after the Lee family, who had recovered the property, sold it to the federal government. Today the cemetery covers 420 acres. Separate monuments to honor the dead of America's wars are centered on the Tomb of the Unknown Soldier, erected in 1931 to commemorate a soldier killed in World War I. Flat stones designate unknowns from more recent wars. Perhaps the most visited site is the grave of John F. Kennedy, marked not with a marble monument but with some of the slain president's favorite plants, a view over the city, and a constantly burning flame. Other members of the Kennedy family are buried nearby.

AND SO MY FELLOW AMERICANS
ASK NOT WHAT YOUR COUNTRY CAN DO FOR YOU
ASK WHAT YOU CAN DO FOR YOUR COUNTRY
MY FELLOW CITIZENS OF THE WORLD · ASK NOT
WHAT AMERICA WILL DO FOR YOU · BUT WHAT TOGETHER
WE CAN DO FOR THE FREEDOM OF MAN

Popularly known as the **Iwo Jima Monument** (left and above), the Marine Corps War Memorial commemorates a decisive moment in World War II.

Dutch friendship with America sounds out in the bells of the **Netherlands Carillon.**

MARINE CORPS WAR MEMORIAL

During the battle for the small Pacific island of Iwo Jima in February 1945 a small detachment of Marines climbed to the island's highest point and planted the American flag. Associated Press photographer Joe Rosenthal, a native Washingtonian, happened to be on hand and arranged for the soldiers to recreate the event for his camera. Instantly famous, the photograph won a Pulitzer Prize later that year. The image inspired Felix W. de Weldon to begin a sculpture of the heroic event. Thirty-six studies preceded de Weldon's completion of the master model in 1951. The faces of the three surviving members of the group were modeled from life; personal photographs aided in modeling the others. Cast in bronze six times life size, the 78-foot-high sculpture was dedicated on November 10, 1954, on the 179th anniversary of the Marine Corps.

NETHERLANDS CARILLON

The site of one of the best views over Washington is occupied by a handsome modernist bell tower given by the people of the Netherlands in gratitude for American aid during and after the second World War. The ring of 49 bells was presented by Queen Juliana in 1952; the steel tower, 127 feet high, was dedicated in 1960. Dutch painter Piet Mondrian's abstract squares and lines seem to be the inspiration for the tower's design. Warm-weather concerts send melodies across the tulips and into the vista beyond.

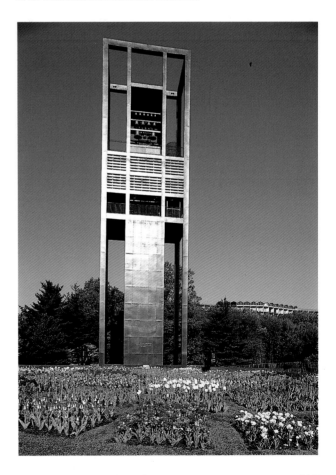

PENTAGON

Built as a command center for America's worldwide military forces during World War II (only the Navy operated out of separate premises), the Pentagon Building remains the headquarters of the Department of Defense. By every statistical measure, this building-within-a-building beggars description: 921 feet on each of the outer building's five sides, 360 feet on each of the inner building's five sides, an outer circumference of 4,605 feet, 7,748 windows, 17,5 miles of corridors, 92 acres of usable office space, 150 stairways, 280 restrooms, 685 drinking fountains, 4,200 installed clocks, 85,000 light fixtures, and parking spaces for 9,500 cars. Authorized by an act of Congress in the middle of the war, in 1941, the building was erected in 1942. It cost $85,000,000. The working population in the building has ranged from 22,718 in 1946, just after the close of World War II, to 31,419 in 1952, during the Korean War. More than 20,000 people—the equivalent of the population of a small city—work there today. The structure's vastness has given rise to a host of legends about people who entered, got lost, and found their way out after days of wandering, among them a messenger boy who entered the building on Friday and emerged on Monday as a lieutenant colonel. The War Department's move from the Old Executive Office Building, via a number of temporary locations, was a move from the largest office building in the world in the nineteenth century to the largest office building in the world in the twentieth century.

*From **the Pentagon** America's military campaigns have been directed since World War II.*

The historic core of one of America's most historic communities is located in Alexandria's **Market Square.**

Houses from the eighteenth and early nineteenth centuries make Alexandria a treasury of American architecture.

ALEXANDRIA

MARKET SQUARE

Founded in 1748, three years before Georgetown, Alexandria was likewise a flourishing tobacco port long before the City of Washington was dreamed of. A youthful George Washington helped lay out the streets of the new town, which soon became the focus of commerce and social activity for the plantations round about, among them Mount Vernon. Market square was the center of it all. On the square's southeastern corner stands the Ramsey House (1749-51), the oldest structure in the city. In a room of the nearby Carlyle House (1752) General Edward Braddock and five royally appointed governors of the colonies met to plan one of major campaigns of the French and Indian War (1753-1763). Next door is the Bank of Alexandria, organized in 1792. At the square's northwestern edge stands Gadsby's Tavern (erected in two stages, 1752 and 1792), which served as George Washington's military headquarters in 1754, when he was lieutenant-colonel of the Virginia Militia, and as the site of his last review of the troops just before his death in 1799.

OLD HOUSES

As federal architecture is Georgetown's distinctive style, so Georgian is Alexandria's. The streets of Old Town are lined with exquisitely detailed townhouses, shops, inns, schools, and churches dating from the late eighteenth and early nineteenth centuries. "Gentry Row" in the 200-block of Prince Street boasts some particularly spectacular examples. One block away the more modest houses of "Captains' Row" tumble down a cobbled street to the Potomac River. Along the waterfront warehouses of the same early period have been converted into shops and restaurants. The Stabler-Leadbeater Apothecary Shop, with its distinctive bow windows, is a rare example of a commercial establishment that has survived virtually unchanged since 1792. There is even a fire-fighting company that traces its origins to 1774. Among several historic churches, the real treasure is Christ Episcopal Church, built between 1767 and 1773. Inside, congregants of today read the Creed and the Lord's Prayer from wall tablets that have never been repainted. The original box pews include those occupied by George Washington's family and Robert E. Lee's.

*A **bronze likeness of Washington** is enshrined within the Masonic National Memorial.*

*The **ancient lighthouse at Alexandria, Egypt,** provided the inspiration for the Masonic Memorial's design.*

MASONIC NATIONAL MEMORIAL

GEORGE WASHINGTON MASONIC NATIONAL MEMORIAL

Riding high atop a site that was once proposed for the U. S. Capitol, the Masonic National Memorial in Alexandria, Virginia, preserves priceless relics associated with George Washington within a building that was designed to recall one of the Seven Wonders of the Ancient World, the lighthouse at Alexandria, Egypt. Like many of the republic's early leaders, George Washington was a Free Mason. He was first master of the Alexandria Lodge, chartered in 1788. Over the years the lodge acquired many pieces of Washington memorabilia, some of which were lost in 1871 when a fire destroyed the lodge's original quarters on Market Square. The remainder are preserved today in a replica of the eighteenth-century lodge room, located within the Masonic National Memorial. On display in the room are the high-back leather chair Washington used while grand master, a pen knife given to him by his mother, his pocket compass, the silver trowel he used to lay the cornerstone of the Capitol, a letter he wrote a few weeks before his death (declining an invitation to a ball), the bleeding instruments used on his deathbed, and the clock from his bedchamber at Mount Vernon, stopped forever at the moment of his death, 10:20 on the evening of December 14, 1799. A pastel portrait of Washington by William Williams of Philadelphia shows the former president six years before his death. Unlike the more famous oil portraits, Williams' likeness of Washington shows an aged man, complete with small-pox scars, a wound on the left cheek, and a mole behind the right ear. Altogether different is the heroic statue of Washington that presides over the Masonic Memorial's grand entrance hall. The cornerstone to the edifice was laid in 1923, using the silver trowel Washington himself had used at the Capitol. Paid for by 3,200,000 Masons throughout the United States, the building was dedicated in 1932. The tower rises 400 feet above the town below and commands a magnificent panorama in all directions.

PREJUDICES AND LOCAL INTERESTS YIELD TO REASON.
LOOK TO OUR NATIONAL CHARACTER AND TO THINGS
OND THE PRESENT PERIOD

G. Washington

The GEORGE WASHINGTON
MASONIC NATIONAL MEMORIAL

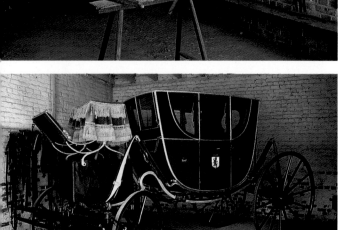

Not only the **mansion house** (above) but outlying buildings and **artefacts of everyday life** (below) make Mount Vernon a museum of colonial America as well as a memorial to America's first president.

MOUNT VERNON

A shrine to the commander in chief of the Revolutionary Army and first President of the United States, Mount Vernon gives visitors a good sense of the agricultural life that George Washington, like many of his peers, left behind when he went to war with Britain and assumed public office. Washington, for one, always longed to get back to the land. The family estate, originally encompassing 5000 acres, had been patented by his ancestor John Washington in 1674. It was George's elder brother Lawrence who started the house that stands today and named it for his old commander, Admiral Edward Vernon of the British navy. The "mount" came naturally enough: the house stands atop a bluff that commands a splendid view of the Potomac. The wide veranda and large cupola that form the house's most distinctive features were added during a major remodeling that George Washington began in 1773. The clapboard siding of the all-wood structure was coated with sand to give the impression of stone blocks. Arched breezeways connect the main house to service buildings that formed, in Washington's day, a self-sustaining country village. Here cotton, wool, and even silk were spun and woven; candles were molded; butter was churned; grapes were pressed and wine was casked; maize and wheat were milled. More than 200 slaves were required to farm the estate and keep it supplied and fed. In his will Washington instructed that the slaves should be freed upon the death of his wife. Near the house a flower garden, planted with eighteenth-century varieties, is laid out according to Washington's original plan. The interior of the main house retains some of the original furnishings. Particularly striking are the large and stylish Banquet Hall, with its Adam-inspired ceiling; the Family Dining Room, where Washington kept open house for a steady stream of visitors; the Library, with the desk and chair Washington used while directing the estate; and the upstairs bedroom containing the bed on which Washington died. In a shady recess down the hillside stands the national hero's simple tomb.

Eighteenth-century gardens (above) and **Washington's tomb** (below) offer opportunities for quiet reflection amid one of America's most visited destinations.

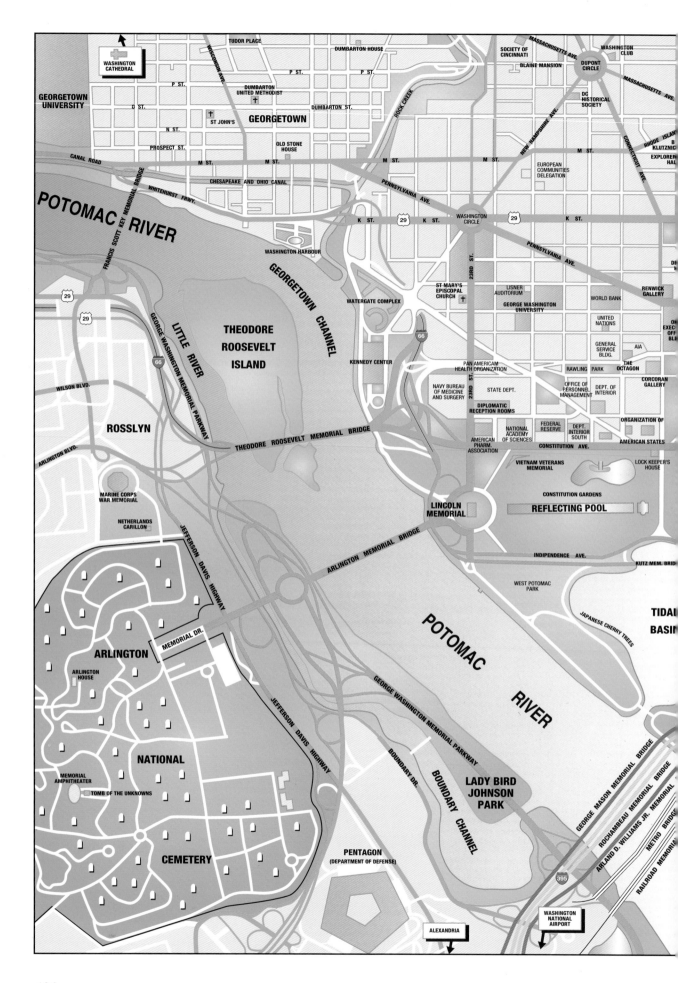

WASHINGTON CATHEDRAL

TUDOR PLACE

DUMBARTON HOUSE

SOCIETY OF CINCINNATI

MASSACHUSETTS AVE.

WASHINGTON CLUB

GEORGETOWN UNIVERSITY

BLAINE MANSION

DUPONT CIRCLE

MASSACHUSETTS AVE.

P ST.

P ST.

P ST.

WISCONSIN AVE.

DUMBARTON UNITED METHODIST

DUMBARTON ST.

NEW HAMPSHIRE AVE.

DC HISTORICAL SOCIETY

RHODE ISLAND

O ST.

ST JOHN'S

GEORGETOWN

CONNECTICUT AVE.

B KLUTZNIC

N ST.

OLD STONE HOUSE

EXPLORER HAL

PROSPECT ST.

M ST.

M ST.

M ST.

M ST.

EUROPEAN COMMUNITIES DELEGATION

CANAL ROAD

M ST.

M ST.

CHESAPEAKE AND OHIO CANAL

PENNSYLVANIA AVE.

WHITEHURST FRWY.

POTOMAC RIVER

FRANCIS SCOTT KEY MEMORIAL BRIDGE

ROCK CREEK

K ST.

29

K ST.

WASHINGTON CIRCLE

29

K ST.

PENNSYLVANIA AVE.

WASHINGTON HARBOUR

23RD ST.

PENNSYLVANIA AVE.

29

GEORGETOWN CHANNEL

ST MARY'S EPISCOPAL CHURCH

LISNER AUDITORIUM

RENWICK GALLERY

DI

29

WATERGATE COMPLEX

GEORGE WASHINGTON UNIVERSITY

WORLD BANK

GEORGE WASHINGTON MEMORIAL PARKWAY

THEODORE ROOSEVELT ISLAND

66

UNITED NATIONS

ON EXEC OFF BLI

LITTLE RIVER

KENNEDY CENTER

GENERAL SERVICE BLDG.

AIA

THE OCTAGON

WILSON BLVD.

66

PAN AMERICAN HEALTH ORGANIZATION

RAWLING PARK

CORCORAN GALLERY

NAVY BUREAU OF MEDICINE AND SURGERY

23RD ST.

STATE DEPT.

OFFICE OF PERSONNEL MANAGEMENT

DEPT. OF INTERIOR

ROSSLYN

DIPLOMATIC RECEPTION ROOMS

ORGANIZATION OF

AMERICAN PHARM. ASSOCIATION

NATIONAL ACADEMY OF SCIENCES

FEDERAL RESERVE

DEPT. INTERIOR SOUTH

AMERICAN STATES

THEODORE ROOSEVELT MEMORIAL BRIDGE

ARLINGTON BLVD.

CONSTITUTION AVE.

VIETNAM VETERANS MEMORIAL

LOCK KEEPER'S HOUSE

MARINE CORPS WAR MEMORIAL

CONSTITUTION GARDENS

NETHERLANDS CARILLON

LINCOLN MEMORIAL

REFLECTING POOL

JEFFERSON DAVIS HIGHWAY

ARLINGTON MEMORIAL BRIDGE

INDIPENDENCE AVE.

KUTZ MEM. BRID

WEST POTOMAC PARK

ARLINGTON

MEMORIAL DR.

POTOMAC

TIDAI

ARLINGTON HOUSE

JAPANESE CHERRY TREES

BASIN

NATIONAL

RIVER

MEMORIAL AMPHITHEATER

JEFFERSON DAVIS HIGHWAY

GEORGE WASHINGTON MEMORIAL PARKWAY

TOMB OF THE UNKNOWNS

BOUNDARY DR.

LADY BIRD JOHNSON PARK

GEORGE MASON MEMORIAL BRIDGE

BOUNDARY CHANNEL

ROCHAMBEAU MEMORIAL BRIDGE

ARLAND D. WILLIAMS JR. MEMORIAL

METRO BRIDGE

CEMETERY

PENTAGON (DEPARTMENT OF DEFENSE)

RAILROAD MEMORIAL

395

WASHINGTON NATIONAL AIRPORT

ALEXANDRIA

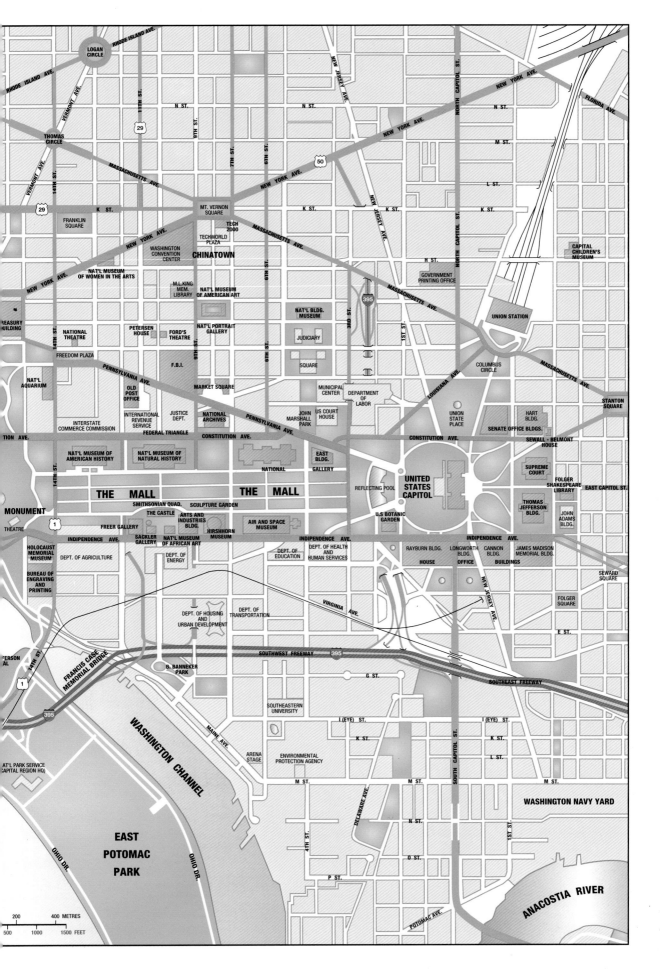

Index